Hospitality

Hospitality

A New Dawn in Sustainability & Service

Chris Sheppardson

BEP

BUSINESS EXPERT PRESS

Leader in applied, concise business books

Hospitality: A New Dawn in Sustainability & Service

Copyright © Business Expert Press, LLC, 2021.

Cover design by Charlene Kronstedt

Interior design by Exeter Premedia Services Private Ltd., Chennai, India

First published in 2021 by
Business Expert Press, LLC
222 East 46th Street, New York, NY 10017
www.businessexpertpress.com

ISBN-13: 978-1-95334-972-9 (paperback)
ISBN-13: 978-1-95334-973-6 (e-book)

Business Expert Press Tourism and Hospitality Management Collection

Collection ISSN: 2375-9623 (print)
Collection ISSN: 2375-9631 (electronic)

First edition: 2021

10 9 8 7 6 5 4 3 2 1

To Mimi and Chessie.

I am so proud of you

There are basically two types of people. People who accomplish things, and people who claim to have accomplished things. The first group is less crowded. (2)

Mark Twain

Description

This book is an introduction to one of the fast developing core pillars in all business, sustainability, as well as how it is tied into the concept of service. Much has changed during the Covid-19 pandemic and we are seeing companies redefine their value propositions with leaders, once again, returning to core basics and beginning to lead through strong pillars.

The new emerging generations are demanding and expecting more. The bar has been raised and the challenge for all leaders is to meet this. There are new leaders emerging with strong visions of the future. As difficult as 2020 has been, we could well be sitting on the brink of a new age in both sustainability and in service. Out of the dark times could come a lot of good but it will require new styles of leadership to what has be seen over the last 20 years.

Keywords

hospitality; sustainability; service; chief executive officer (CEO); managing director (MD); human resources director (HRD); millennials; Gen Z; BAME; diversity; C-suite; food; culture; economic; environmental; social; society; mergers & acquisitions (M&A); hotels; food service; restaurants; chefs; cuisine

Contents

Prologue xi

Introduction xvii

Chapter 1   How Economic Sustainability Lost Its Way 1

Chapter 2   Sustainable Business 13

Chapter 3   Social Renewal 41

Chapter 4   Cultural Sustainability 55

Chapter 5   Change to the Work Place 71

Chapter 6   Sustainability Through Food 89

Chapter 7   The Cousins—Sustainability and Service 105

Chapter 8   Nothing Is More Important Than Trust and
             Relationships 123

Chapter 9   An Industry of Hope and Optimism, One Which
             Can Break Barriers 131

Chapter 10   Service Is purpose 141

References 145

About the Author 151

Index 153

Prologue

We must accept finite disappointment, but we must never lose infinite hope.

Martin Luther King, Jr. (1)

The last 20 years has seen many challenges from the Great Crash of 2008/09 to the Covid-19 pandemic crisis as well as a new generation struggle to break through and another reluctant to leave the stage. These challenges have had their consequences, good and bad. The Great Crash arguably set back many progressive agendas and the pandemic crisis may just mark a moment of reset. Time will tell whether this becomes a truth. The following book though is an explanation of the journey that many companies have travelled during the last few decades, the ups and downs, the setbacks and the progress, until we have reached a point where we can see a more progressive era lie within touching distance. This is the story of that journey.

Most moments of real change require a catalyst, a moment in time which makes change inevitable. It is often argued that change cannot be created without the natural "comfort zone" in which people live being removed. Genuine hardship creates a momentum for change; war, poverty, abuse, and fear. The interesting question to ask about the last decade is that as the world has never been safer, so has that safety hindered the change that has been desired and needed? Have all not strived hard enough to create the need for change that so many want and talk about? Have we all not walked the words we talk?

Many believe that the Covid-19 pandemic could mark such a moment in time. Many certainly believe that we are sitting on the brink of a new era which will have a strong central pillar built around the principle of sustainability.

The concept of "sustainability" is too often linked to issues of environmental impact when the truth is that it is also about a business's impact on society, on culture, and on economics. Environment is naturally of major importance but so are our cultures, society, and economies. There has been a drive toward globalization which has also made many yearn for localism. Can both live alongside one another effectively?

During the pandemic, many companies have found their structures to be wanting, vulnerable, and less effective than was expected. There is a genuine need for stronger roots to be grown. Many blame the increased activity in M&A and by venture capitalists, both resulting in more narrow thinking and less investment in the roots of a culture, in values, and in leadership. Is this true and fair?

There is a growing belief that out of the dark times in 2020 could come a renewed, stronger approach toward service, people, community, and culture and in building stronger businesses.

There are many who have felt frustrated and disappointed by the slow progress made in sustainability over the last 10 years. The feeling is that economics and business plans have often been short-term focused in approach, which has hindered any real progress. It has also been felt, rightly or wrongly, that too many companies have verbally supported sustainability agendas but not in real action or investment. It has resulted in feeling frustration in the lack of progress across all four pillars of sustainability—economic, environmental, social, and cultural. There are hundreds of articles making a case for stronger actions.

It has taken time but there are signs of a genuine change not just in action but in mindset. An interesting comment was recently made during an informal conversation:

> You should no longer not just think about how you serve your guest, but on how you impact on the lives of the community around.

It would be easy to assume that the comment was said by a leading hospitality executive but in fact it was said by a senior player from a leading financial institution. It reflects the sea change in mindset which is taking place where companies now understand that they cannot just operate as a silo but have a role to play in something which is bigger and can be more influential. The aforementioned senior player was describing his belief that a company does need today to possess high aspirations in how it behaves, both to their clients and to the community in which it sits. The younger, emerging generations are asking for better behaviors and higher aspirations. As they quietly move into positions of influence, a momentum of change is gradually building.

In conversation, the aforementioned financier went on to say

One of the biggest shifts has been an understanding that we were consistently losing respect because we were seen to be untrustworthy. Of course, this meant that we would lose clients and not be able to attract the best talent that we wanted. It was a hard realisation. It did remind me of the Conservative Party (in the UK) back in about 2002 when they openly accepted that they were seen as "The Nasty Party". It took The Conservatives five years to accept this reality and then another seven or eight years to become electable. It has probably taken us more than a single decade to accept and it may take another decade to win back real trust but that is the journey we have to begin. Expectations are rightly higher today than they have been before.

He does not sit alone. Many C-Suite executives are working hard to lead real cultural change within their businesses. There is a widespread acceptance that a lot of the problems which have evolved over the past 10 years have been as a result of poor leadership and poor behaviors. Too many companies did give up on investing in their cultures, in their missions and core purpose, and in their people in order to create models which registered the best results that they could. There are many CEOs and MDs who are now working hard to ensure that their business teams do start reinvesting back, not just in people, but the purpose of the company, the meaning of the company, its values, culture, and messaging. Profit is the result of a strong mission and purpose which brings all the stakeholders together rather than just being the sole purpose at all costs.

It marks a shift in mindset, an aspiration back to believing in something bigger, where leadership teams understand that they need to connect once again with their customers and with their employees through having a purpose which does embrace the sustainability agenda. Many harbor great hopes that we will see an emergence of greater care, compassion, and commitment toward communities, society, in business, and in the environment.

It could well be that we do sit at the start of an exciting new era, the brink of a new age where a strong balance between all four pillars (economic, social, cultural, and environmental) will stand far closer together and once again become central features in business strategies. This is important to be achieved as it will also serve to heal the gulf between generations, rebuild trust in leaders and in the actions of companies.

The last decade has seen a gradual but deep erosion in trust in the relationship between employees and employer; between customers and company; between society and business. It is regularly argued that thinking has been too internalized with not enough thought given to customers who create the revenue flows, to employees, and to local communities in which the business operates.

Why Is Change Now Taking Place?

Ever since the middle of the last decade, the business case for stronger sustainable businesses has become louder and stronger as the cost of implementation has fallen, and new technology has come forward. The issue has moved from sitting on the periphery, only as far back as 2010, to becoming a central issue in the development of strategies. It may have taken 30 years to reach this point, but this just highlights how long it does take to create genuine change. A whole re-education was needed, and it does take a long time to change attitudes and behaviors. One only has to review the many Hollywood films arguing the case for environmental sustainability dating back to the start of the 1990s. Even with this energy and power behind the need for change, it has felt remarkably slow.

Today, investors as well as the emerging generations understand the value of building sustainable business. Companies need investors onside and naturally, great young talent does have higher expectations too. To compete for leading talent, companies do need to show genuine commitment toward the sustainability agenda. Losing both would cause major problems so change is inevitable. The challenge is to ensure that this momentum is here to stay, especially as companies rebuild after Covid-19, and that the foundations now laid will be built upon. It is easy to high-light how the "Great Crash" of 2008/09 did not lead to the change in behaviors so often debated between 2008 to 2010 but rather led to a more controlled business environment which hindered progressive agendas.

The drive of investors and of the emerging generations together will force leadership teams to think more broadly and differently. Both will want to see stronger care for society and for the environment.

At the same time, the millennial generation has come to force as the largest group in employment. They have felt disappointed in the last decade by the leadership they have experienced, and they have a desire for better. They are the most educated, diverse, and inclusive generation to emerge as yet and they are making the case for greater change. They have strong ideals and they are coming into positions of influence. The chances are that greater progress will be inevitable.

The Baby Boom generation has been one of the finest business gen-erations but they have faced a lot of criticism in how they have struggled to nurture the millennials through. Some of this has been fair; some not so. The irony is the millennials are a reflection of the Baby Boomers, just their private or home selves. In truth, there is far less difference than one expects from the narrative which is commonly heard. Both generations possess strong values. The key difference is that the Baby Boomers really broke through during the 1980s in a less wealthy, yet freer social environ-ment, so all understood that they would need to compromise on some values to ensure financial stability. They had to fight for security. Most western societies are wealthier today, stronger and safer. Therefore, the need to compromise on ideals is less pronounced and the millennials have been quietly advocating a need for change. They want to see greater focus on business having stronger senses of purpose and mission.

One can hardly argue that the millennials have been loud voices. They have been very respectful but there is no doubting their desire to see genuine change. As a result, they have been noticeably disengaged and less loyal to what has often been viewed as poor leadership. They were brought up to believe in better and they want to live their lives living up to those values.

The key difference was simply a question of the progressive position of society. The 1960s did witness genuine progress but it was a harsher time.

The 1970s was a tough economic period but also a period when many societies felt that progress did stagnate. The 1980s became an era where upward social mobility and wealth creation were the dominant themes and of course, these were the years in which the Baby Boomers entered the workplace.

As noted, the Baby Boomers started themselves with strong idealism and they broke many barriers as did the previous generation, the so-called Silent Generation. It was the Silent Generation which was fully active, crying out for change, during the 1960s and 1970s as the Baby Boomers were still working their way through their formative and teenage years. The parents of the Silent Generation must have struggled with the behaviors of their children, through Woodstock and the "love" revolution of the 1960s, far more than the Baby Boomers have had to struggle with the millennial generation which has been far more quiet and respectful. Arguably, the millennials have been too respectful, neither fought for the change they desired nor have they challenged leaders more actively which is why Baby Boomers have continued to lead as they see fit, without enough pressure from emerging leaders.

However, both the Silent Generation and the Baby Boomer generation have parented with greater levels of love, care, and education than those before. They have laid the land for change but it will be the next generations who see this change through.

Generations have traditionally critiqued each other over the years but it is the compromises made and the wealth generated over the last 40 years which have laid the ground for real change to come. The Silent Generation and the Baby Boomers have laid the ground for a potentially stronger environment to emerge.

The world faces some serious problems in how it rebuilds after the pandemic. It will need a genuine philosophy of change to create the momentum needed. Trust needs to be rebuilt and there is a growing desire amongst the emerging generations for a philosophy of collaboration, working far better as communities and in service of others. The signs are that a new momentum is building, and it could well be that we stand at the start of a new era.

However, will rebuilding economies and business after Covid-19 see this become even stronger or fall back again?

Introduction

The Importance of Sustainability in Building Toward the Future

One of the underlying narratives during the Covid pandemic is that it has allowed for many to have time for reflection, to rediscover core values, and to create an impetus to fast-forward the need for change. One of the most dominant discussions has been the challenge to re-engage employees, of all ages, to return to offices.

Strangely, it has not just been middle-level executives who have been reluctant to return to the office but also many senior players including C-Suite level. It has not been as simplistic to place this all down to the risk of Covid; there are far deeper issues involved which also include a deep frustration over how negative many work environments have become. This is not a new issue, and a momentum had already been building, before the crisis, that a change was needed. Business and work environments had become staid, uninspiring and demanded longer hours. There were lessons which needed to be heard.

There are a number of key learnings to emerge from the Covid-19 crisis and maybe the most important is that many have found something of genuine importance in how communities have reconnected and collaborated together. At the heart of it lies the fact that during lockdown and the crisis, many have had time for more face-to-face interactions which have arguably led to improved behaviors, compassion, friendship, and productivity.

One company recently researched its employees and was shocked to discover that 70 percent did not wish to return to the office. Another recently noted that their own C-Suite were reluctant to return until later in the year.

Many employees, across all sectors, have noted that they have lacked trust in the effectiveness and behaviors in that have been leading. Many want to see greater mission and purpose; strong values; more genuine, kinder behaviors; and greater commitment to wider issues.

There are a number of key learnings to emerge from the Covid-19 crisis and maybe the most important is that many have found something of genuine importance in how communities have reconnected and collaborated together. At the heart of it lies the fact that during lockdown and the crisis, many have had time for more face-to-face interactions, seen personal contact and relationships once again come to prominence; all which have arguably led to improved behaviors, compassion, friendship, and productivity.

During this period, many have reconnected with values that are important to them. They have connected again with friends, neighbors, local communities, and the local environment and they don't want to lose this connection. Many want to get back to the basics, their companies providing a real service level which impacts positively.

Things will not just go back to as it was. Companies are going to have to adapt and make sure their own processes are stronger and that they do have a mission and sense of purpose which is more than just generating profit. There is a push back against automated services, business arrogance toward customers, against the advancement in process, combined with a desire to make people feel once again valued and cared for through designed service focused on the guest. People and service are once again being seen to be of real importance.

There is a mindset shift taking place and it will mean that companies will need to create new thinking in HR, in corporate social responsibility (CSR), in marketing, in communications, in leadership, and in service.

One leading hotelier recently remarked in an interview with *EP Magazine* (2a) that:

Too many hoteliers think about things too narrowly. They see the guest as almost a transaction rather than thinking through the customer experience. There has been a greater and greater focus on the asset value which is all fine but hotels are also about delivering a service. One of the problems is that in the last ten years valuations have gone up which has made the small operational issues seem of less importance.

Guests though want to feel special. They want to be wowed. Teams want to deliver service of excellence. Running a hotel is a special privilege as it provides the opportunity to really do something that makes the guest feel important and for them then to value you.

Profit is the sum of a lot of small parts coming together to do something special. Building a great hotel is about getting those small parts right.

Out of all this, there is a growing belief that business will go back and get their basic foundations right again and this could see the start of a new progressive age, a broader and more enlightened approach to business in a number of areas. We could well be sitting at the start of a new golden era which does, once again, find a stronger balance between business, environment, society, and customers. However, there is still much to be done, a journey to be travelled and to overcome which can still happen to hinder progress.

All in all, business needs to set stronger roots in the ground so it can build effectively.

It is no accident that this has come to the fore. It has been building for some time, from before the crisis struck. Many have blamed social media for many of the woes and the erosion of trust but the real truth is that the issues are more closely aligned to an erosion in face-to-face interactions, longer work hours, increased pressures, and a decline in strong cultures/values within business. There is no little research to support this perspective.

- A 2018 study, by Cigna, found that close to half of all Americans feel alone and isolated. The study suggests that the use of technology and social media has minimal influence on a person's feelings of isolation. The study found that it was the decline of face-to-face interactions which had the most impact.

- People are craving community now more than ever. For businesses, this means that creating a strong community, of clients and employees, is critical to success. For hospitality, it can also play a central role in bringing people together within companies and within communities.
- Many believe that eating together creates greater understanding and breaks down barriers.
- Many also argue that informal communications have declined within business along with a decline in face-to-face contact, which together have made performance less effective.
- During Covid-19, many have found stronger relationships within their own communities rather than from work colleagues. In an interview with *EP Magazine*, the leading hotelier Carrie Wicks (2b) spoke of how the lockdown saw her London street neighbors all come together and support each other as never before. They had lived their lives without knowing each other and now they had the time to share time and find friendships. It created a renewed sense of community which many found pleasure in.

It is not a hard case to make to say that if a company wants to build strong performance, then it will need to once again build a strong community, a real connection with employees and with customers.

What does this all mean?

- Communications strategies will move from talking almost predominantly about a brand to a focus on community to increase brand awareness, understand customers, improve outcomes, build trust, and develop greater loyalty. Despite all the advances in modern communications, the most effective way to raise awareness and grow a business is through word-of-mouth. It is stated that 84 percent are likely to trust a referral or recommendation if it comes from a friend, meaning the importance of community is at an all-time high.

- There is a desire for greater celebration of regional customs, traditions, histories, food styles, and produce.
- Creating communities should be a primary area of focus in all local and business strategies.
- For hospitality, there is a genuine real opportunity to step forward and bring people together—in business, in schools, in daily life—to improve face-to-face interactions, improve communications and trust, and break down barriers.

There has been a genuine shift in how many companies and their leadership teams think on the issues of sustainability as well as a refocusing on service, with boards beginning to place people back at the heart of many strategies.

These have been areas of genuine concern in the past decade where many believed that little was done, more than the sounding of good intentions. It has become almost a cliché that many are tired of tick box approach by companies toward CSR. More is being quietly demanded. Since 2015, there has been a genuine change in the sustainability narrative, and with each passing year more real action materializes.

Many will argue that the Covid-19 crisis would have been a catalyst for genuine change, but the truth is that change was already demanded and actively in progress. The Covid-19 crisis has just helped push the need for change to a faster pace.

The emergence of the millennial generation and Gen Z in the business environment has increased the call for stronger and higher standards in business. Investors too are seeking more actual evidence of strategies which impact positively on sustainability.

The world has woken up to sustainability and hotels need to be seen walking the talk and leading by example.
—Marc Dardenne, CEO, Luxury Brands Europe, Accor

The relative inaction on sustainability during the years 2010 to 2015 were a frustration. The counter is that many economies needed to retrench after the 2008/09 crash and rebuild strength. It was, therefore, natural that some agendas needed to take a backward step, and that was often sustainability.

There are those who argue that many good things happened during these years, and to a certain extent, this is true, but it was more in specific pockets. The London 2012 Olympics were reported to be the greenest on record and the event's food service approach did set new benchmarks in sustainability. At the heart of the London Olympics stood a strong social philosophy to regenerate a poor area of London, to inspire the young generations to better lives and to ensure a truly sustainable approach to the Olympic Park's development. The event was an undoubted success story, which created ripples of change. It set new and higher levels of aspiration in environmental sustainability. It created a belief in revitalizing local social infrastructures and even more so, it convinced a skeptical host nation that it could really host great events at a world-class level. It created a genuine psychological belief which went on to be seen further with the Rugby World Cup of 2015 and the Cricket World Cup in 2019. However, the Olympics was a global event that presented London to a global audience. It was not everyday business. It set new benchmarks for excellence which inspired other actions, even though it took time for that inspiration to filter through.

The core argument has been that the recovery from the Great Recession of 2008/09 set back any real progress to sustainability; that both economies and businesses needed to rebuild and understandably placed this at the top of agendas. This is true but, as is so often the case, only part of the picture.

It was the financial sector that felt the brunt of the fallout from the great crash of 2008/09. It was however those in middle- and lower-level incomes that felt the full force of the fallout. Surprisingly, there was very little change within the board room. Stability became the very clear mantra and the emphasis was on ensuring the business focused less on progressive strategies and more on strong economics. This argument held merit to shareholders in the early part of the last decade but as time progressed, so there has been a growing demand for stronger and improved behaviors in sustainability and within society. It has taken time, but the business case for sustainability has been gradually made and there is a genuine energy in seeing companies being far more progressive in both word and deed.

> Sustainability has become considered to be a key operational deliverable. New developments from design construction and operation are incorporating effective principles which customers today not just expect, but demand.
>
> —John Murphy, Executive VP, EFM Hospitality

There is a new generation emerging which has been relatively quiet and respectful. They have listened, often felt disappointed, and waited for their opportunity. They are better educated than any previous generation, see less barriers to upward social mobility, in gender and in race. They have arguably been the generation which has been most adversely affected by the fallout in 2008/09. They have faced adversity and they do possess the energy to see real change take place. They also believe in the importance of communities to a greater extent than the Baby Boom generation. They have lost faith in leadership from the top and instead opted to find leadership which is more local and more personal. This can help explain the #MeToo campaign which was, in many ways, a rebellion against the behaviors of the old school. It also helps to explain why the "Black Lives Matter" campaign took off with such energy during the height of the pandemic crisis in 2020.

However, interestingly there are real splits across society today: those who really support the so-called "Woke" agendas, those in the media and liberal elitist bubble who often seem disconnected from the average person, those who have become increasingly disengaged from liberalism and agendas, and those who do focus on what will impact on their communities. The last group has a desire for a stronger social normality and community. Although there is a natural gulf between the liberal elite and the mainstream populations, there is far less of a gulf between generations as is sometimes portrayed.

Many have painted a picture of conflict between the Baby Boomers and the millennials but the truth is that the latter is simply a reflection of the former, not in business but at home.

Baby Boomers have long been a bit of a Jekyll and Hyde personality, full of strong ideals but so often quick to place wealth first and compromise accordingly. Many historians will probably point to the psychological effect of a tougher decade in the 1970s, the social unrest and violence, the protests and cynicism that arguably built a hunger for personal security which was then released in the 1980s under the Ronald Reagan–Margaret Thatcher ideologies which saw a philosophy that encouraged a higher level of self-interest and entrepreneurial spirit.

However, the Baby Boomers grew up with great idealism and would often, in their younger days, be found on protest marches and talking with great passion on social injustice. This was nothing new. The Silent Generation had set the tone in the 1960s. The difference is only that they grew up in a harsher age and they focused on building wealth to get away from those days. But did they create the greater social justice they believed in? Maybe not but they did lay the land for a new generation which can build on their work.

As Abigail Tan, CEO of the St. Giles Hotel Group, noted in an interview, there is far less of a difference between the generations than is sometimes portrayed:

"This gap has emerged because we have a multi-generational workforce at the same time when our world is experiencing a fast-paced cultural evolution," commented Abigail in the interview for this book.

> On one hand you have young Matures and Baby Boomers seeing a world that they helped create undergo an almost complete transformation. On the other hand, we have the Millennial generation who are natives to this fast-paced cultural shift. Therefore, it may seem that these generations have a clash in values and expectations, but like most things, when we delve further, we see there are fewer differences than what's perceived. When the gap is bridged or the perspective shifts, we tend to see transformation leadership.

The issue is far less about generational difference but that our greatest barrier is our own understanding. Too often, our broader perspectives have become compromised by the immediate challenges that we face and the information we are given. More often than not, thinking has been too narrow and actions not enough to create a lasting impact.

A very good colleague who worked for the United Nations in Africa would often argue that sometimes we need to strive harder to understand the perspectives of others: that our own education is sometimes not enough. He would often argue that there was a gulf between perception and reality. Too often the advanced nation's perceptions of Africa were often simplistic and misguided at best.

If one goes back to 30 years ago, Africa was portrayed as the world's basket case, its territories and people objectified as "needing to be helped." Africa's story was mostly told primarily by foreign correspondents who would parachute in as conflicts erupted. The news window for African stories was limited, and the stories of choice highlighted famine, disaster, powerlessness, displaced populations on the move, and despots taking advantage of their people.

However, Africa has also long been a continent of very rich resources and developing at no little speed, despite what many would write. Africa has moved, in relative terms, very swiftly from being a "basket case" to being a continent of real economic potential. The problem is that many just did not see the change in emphasis or understood the substance behind the story.

It was by the dawn of the new century that the narrative had evolved a long way from one of a "hopeless continent" which was often portrayed during the 1970s, 1980s, and 1990s to one of a buoyant, rising Africa replete with opportunities for investors and populated by a burgeoning middle class bound to become model consumers and fuel economic growth. African economies started to grow steadily, by an average of 5 percent from 2000 onwards, buoyed by stronger governance, more prudent economic stewardship, and consistently high prices for commodities.

Nigeria makes the case. Nigeria is described as "a middle-income, mixed economy and emerging market, with expanding manufacturing, financial, service, communications, technology and entertainment sectors." It is ranked as the 27th largest economy in the world in terms of GDP and the 22nd in terms of purchasing power parity.

According to a Citigroup report published in February 2011, Nigeria will have the highest average GDP growth in the world between 2010 and 2050 (4). Nigeria is one of two countries from Africa among 11 global growth generation countries. Goldman Sachs too wrote of how Nigeria could become one of the world's economic powerhouses in times to come. It has arguably changed dramatically over a 30-year period.

The message is very simple; often our own understanding creates our own barriers to being able to see a different picture. How many times have we all been let down by our own perceptions which have been found to be wanting? In the modern environment, we often do not have an open mind to the changes which are taking place all around us. Arguably with so much more information at our fingertips today we trust our instincts less and our thinking has become increasingly narrow.

Why is this Relevant?

The Nigeria example illustrates how much perceptions have changed in just 30 years. Back in the mid-1990s, there was a strong awareness across advanced economies of the challenges posed by both environmental and social issues. It was well known in that period of time that real actions would need to take place in order to generate real change. The environment was a major concern. It was also known that more needed to be done to help promote the causes of both women and black, Asian, and minority ethnic (BAME) talents and it was well known that there were major social issues which needed to be confronted.

Twenty-five years on and the debate is still taking place. The difference is that these issues have moved from the periphery to the core. One could argue that they should have been central for the last 25 years, and even though they were, it is clear that not enough action has taken place for real progress. Or perhaps is that simply the length of time that it takes to make an argument and create change?

One can waste time arguing about the failures of the past but the real focus should be on the challenges and progression intended for the future. In preparation for this book, 100 senior players were interviewed and it is clear that both the issues of sustainability and people are today central in the thinking of leadership teams. It may have taken 25 or 30 years, but it is now on the board table and there is genuine hope for a brighter future.

Perhaps the lesson is that it does take 30 years in order to re-educate an ingrained belief. Maybe this is one of the keys to the future as the pace of change gets ever faster; that listening, learning, and exploring new thinking is more important than the traditional beliefs that one may have been raised with. Many today will talk that leadership is changing from being the traditional directorial approach to one of listening and adapting to the very uncertain and vulnerable world evolving around them.

The Opportunity for Hospitality

There is also a great opportunity for the hospitality industry on a number of levels. Hospitality is, and has always been, a reflection of society. It can play a leading role in environmental sustainability and this will be important as it will potentially determine investment as well as customer loyalty. More and more customers are now purchasing products where sustainability is clearly of importance.

> Customers have more awareness and they will be choosing a hotel based on a sustainability approach. Hotels can be a fantastic platform to showcase what hospitality can do for the planet and our commitment to society. Hotels can lead the future.
> —Luc De la Fosse, Vice President Hospitality, Al Khozama
> Management Company

However, there is a bigger piece to the jigsaw: the role it can play in supporting social and cultural sustainability in those that it employs, the suppliers that it works with, and moreover the story that it can tell of the community that surrounds the hotels. Leading hotels often talk to global audiences. They should not sit alone, as many do, isolated from the community which surrounds them. Customers do today seek not just stronger and greater experiences but also to almost "feel and touch" the historical story of the society in which a hotel sits. Hotels can represent and tell the cultural story in a very effective way which then also supports the local community.

One senior Scottish hotelier always noted that when guests visited his hotel they wanted to be greeted by a Scot in a kilt at the door and a Scot on reception. It was all part of the expected experience. This has always been true. However, it can go deeper with a story of the local history which encourages guests to explore the locality, try local cuisines, visit restaurants, and appreciate local crafts.

The desire of many today is that there is greater collaboration and care across society: that a hotel or restaurant does not sit as a silo but plays a role for the broader community. Hotels and restaurants have a major social role to play. They can be community leaders, and this is good for business as it naturally builds strength through local advocacy and support.

It is the same with the talent that hospitality employs. It is often one of the primary employers in any location and how it behaves toward minority groups can be crucial. The world has moved on from the bad old days and today, most understand the value that many minority and migrant groups have had on local economies. One of the most exciting aspects of the emergence of the new generations is that they are better educated and see far fewer barriers in gender or race. All these issues need to be removed once and for all, for all talent to have equal opportunities and for the industry to find genuine pride in its ability to be a meritoc-racy where anyone, regardless of their background, can build a successful career.

One of the questions frequently asked is whether many resorts and major hotels have understood the real role that they can and should play in representing the historical story and culture of a community? Today's travellers and customers are looking for something deeper, for more gen-uine, authentic experiences that do connect them to the culture and com-munity that they are visiting. Hotels can be the stage that can tell the story and showcase local customs which in turn, of course, support the economics of many local communities. A real bond can be found once again between communities and hotels. Both can support the other. Both can represent the other. All businesses today have a major role to play in the communities within which they operate. Business today can play a public service role which has arguably been missing through politics.

Hospitality has an important role to play both in environment and in society. This could be a progressive new age.

The Power of Service

What is it that really makes a difference in how any customer feels toward a hotel or any given service they receive? What is it that builds loyalty and trust?

Just as there is a new age potentially coming to the fore in sustainability, so the same is true in relation to service. Businesses, across all disciplines, are suddenly working harder to once again build a personal and stronger relationship with their customers. There has been a realization just how many have been left frustrated and agitated by call centers and automated services. The Edelman Trust Barometer in January 2020, before the Covid-19 crisis, declared that:

> The 2020 Edelman Trust Barometer reveals that despite a strong global economy and near full employment, none of the four societal institutions that the study measures—government, business, NGOs and media—is trusted. The cause of this paradox can be found in people's fears about the future and their role in it, which are a wake-up call for our institutions to embrace a new way of effectively building trust: balancing competence with ethical behaviour…more than half of respondents globally believe that capitalism in its current form is now doing more harm than good in the world…less than half of the mass population trust their institutions to do what is right. (3a)

Given the aforementioned, it is clear that businesses do need to work harder if they truly wish to possess a strong customer base and strong recommendations.

In a world where trust has been in gradual decline for a long time, little is more important than to once again build personal relationships and trust. A couple of thoughts as we open the book:

- If you were hosting a dinner party and you did not welcome a guest personally and with warmth, if you did not go the extra mile to make them feel welcome in your own home, are you surprised if the relationship does not grow? If the answer is "of course not," then why is it different in business?

- Too often investment in service is seen to be a cost rather than part of an economic purpose to exceed a customer's expectations and build loyalty. In truth why? Do you believe that shortcuts can be created, if you wish to build service excellence?
- Is the very basis of service excellence the desire to exceed expectation? If so, when was the last time you witnessed such service and what is your impression of that organization?
- How many operations reflect the growing desire for pride in local culture, gastronomy, and history? The real roots of French Gastronomy lies in regional and local cooking. It has never been a trend or fashion: it is something real, genuine, and authentic; and each area is proud of their regional cooking and wine. It lies within the soul of each region. It is no coincidence that France is the most visited country in the world.

More and more people, across all walks of life, are disengaged by the mainstream: by mainstream news reporting, by the media, by liberal or conservative elites and the so-called "Woke" agendas, by leaders, and by institutions and are turning to both global and local agendas. They are seeking something of greater meaning where they can find both purpose and trust. If a business wants to build trust once again, the service and genuine human contact sits right at the heart of the way forward. It really does matter. It was Michael Gray, a former VP with Hyatt in the United Kingdom, who noted that:

We used to think of guests coming to our home, but our thinking changed when we learnt that we were entering the guest's lives and playing a role.

What role do you want your business to play in a guest or customer's life? This is the question to be discussed.

CHAPTER 1

How Economic Sustainability Lost Its Way

There has been a growing voice for business to have a central focus, in its strategies, on building stronger pillars in both sustainability and service within businesses. This is not just related to environmental sustainability but also in terms of social sustainability, in culture, in business ethics, in economics, in the management of human capital, and in creating once again a connection between the customer and a company. It is a very broad and wide-reaching agenda which will naturally challenge the focus of many businesses in recent years. Many customers today want to know that they are associating themselves with a brand or business which will contribute to the benefits of society.

There are a number of key learnings to emerge from the Covid-19 crisis and maybe the most important is that many have found something of genuine importance in how communities have reconnected and collaborated together. At the heart of it lies the fact that during "lockdowns" and the pandemic, many have had time for more face-to-face interactions which have arguably led to improved behaviors, compassion, friendship, and productivity.

During this period, many have reconnected with values that are important to them. They have connected again with friends, neighbors, local communities, and local environment and they don't want to lose this connection. Many want to get back to the basics; to see their companies providing a real service level which impacts positively.

Things will not just go simply back to as it was. Companies are going to have to adapt and make sure their own processes are stronger, that they do have a mission and sense of purpose which is more than just generating profit. There is a pushback, from consumers, against automated services, business arrogance toward customers, increased processes combined with a desire to make people feel once again valued and cared for through designed service focused on the guest. People and service are once again being seen to be of real importance.

Out of all this, there is a growing belief that business will refocus and get their basic foundations right once again. This could see the start of a new progressive age, a broader and more enlightened approach to business in a number of areas. It could be the start of a new golden era which does find a stronger balance between business, environment, society, and customers. However, there is still much to be done, a journey to be traveled and to overcome, which can still happen to hinder progress. All in all, business needs to set stronger roots in the ground so it can build effectively.

In terms of sustainability, this voice has been steadily growing for over thirty years. The last decade seems to have been a time when the argument has moved from the periphery to becoming a core piece. The great hotelier, Ken McCulloch, founder of Malmaison and Dakota Hotels, would often comment:

> Too many hoteliers see the guest as almost a transaction rather than thinking through the customer experience. Guests want to feel special. They want to be wowed and one does has to look through their eyes to understand the experience. Running a hotel is a special privilege as it provides the opportunity to really do something that makes the guest feel important and for them then to value you.
>
> Many hoteliers talk about their figures but profit is the sum of a lot of small parts coming together to do something special. Building a great hotel is about getting those small parts right.

We could see the start of a new progressive age, a new dawn, with a broader and more enlightened approach to business. We could well be sitting at the start of a new golden era which does, once again, find a stronger balance between business, environment, society, and customers. However, there is still much to be done, a journey to be taken and to overcome, which carries many dangers and much can still happen to hinder progress.

Many will argue that the Covid-19 crisis has been a catalyst for great change and to a degree this is true but the pressure on change was already steadily growing over-the last decade. Change was already in the making. The Covid-19 crisis may help cement the argument but in truth, it is probably just been a period which allowed many to reflect and review what they believed in.

There has been a growing level of discontent with the practices of many businesses, a declining trust in many leaders, a growing frustration over-what many have seen as a "tick-box" approach to CSR and sustainability with no real action. There has also been a growing frustration in the fact that many women have not broken through to board level as well as the lack of BAME in senior positions. All this has created a gradual erosion in the commitment of many younger talents who want to see higher standards in behaviors and a far more progressive approach to business.

It will be interesting to review how historians write about the years 2008 to 2020 and how kind they will be to those in leadership roles. When the financial crash of 2008/09 took place, many noted that it would be a time to learn key lessons, that leaders would need to learn from the errors made. At the time, it was described as a major heart attack to the system which would create the basis of corrections. Behaviors had changed with the long financial boom and unfortunately, values had been eroded. Prime Minister Gordon Brown commented that:

> The motto of the old order in the City of London was, "My word is my bond," but the financial crisis revealed a culture quite alien to that heritage. The stewards of people's money were revealed to have been speculators with it. (5)

Steve Bannon commented that:

> My old firm, Goldman Sachs—traditionally, the best banks are leveraged 8:1. When we had the financial crisis in 2008, the investment banks were leveraged 35:1. Those rules had specifically been changed by a guy named Hank Paulson. He was secretary of Treasury. (6)

As indicated earlier it was the financial sectors which took the brunt of the criticism. Business faced a turbulent period with the "age of austerity" being announced, but were any lessons from the 2008/09 crash learnt? Did the values of those in leadership teams change and adapt in response to the crisis?

Arguably, many behaviors actually declined further. Many directors protected themselves during the fallout and it was the lower- and middle-income level employees who faced the worst. Lost employees were replaced with automated systems; business processes and the gap between the wealth of senior players and those in middle management actually got greater. Research shows that the remuneration of senior players during this time doubled whilst the relative remuneration of middle management only grew by between 25 percent and 30 percent in the same period. The argument was that senior players were being rewarded via greater bonuses on business results and returns to the shareholder: a fair argument even if one dimensional. They were being incentivized to deliver greater profit, but at what cost?

It would naturally lead to increased self-interest and one-dimensional thinking which focused almost solely on results. Even if this was understandable to rebuild from the crash, it was clearly not a long-term, sustainable approach. The increased activity by venture capitalists and M and A activity has attracted blame for this but of course, this is simplistic. Business models focused on shareholder returns to a higher level and the core roots a business needs were not invested in strongly enough. It became an accepted reality from time back to the late 1990s to reduce spend in key "soft" disciplines in return for higher net margin, regardless of the consequence.

The response has often been one of genuine surprise in recent years over-some of the statistics to emerge over-the disengagement of employees and the erosion in trust in leadership teams. There are many who will still dispute the rise in stress, anxiety, and mental illness. Many others genuinely reject the levels of disengagement as being almost a lack of character or a lack of ambition and drive. However, the growing disengagement is then surely a natural evolution from the aforementioned?

Maybe one of the best ways to illustrate the point is the change which has taken place across the human resources function over-the years.

Many are critical of their HR teams but the role has changed from having a genuine focus on the human asset as the role was originally designed to be to becoming an almost legal and technical function. The result has been an erosion in trust, a decline in focus on culture and on the development of talent. Business has moved to becoming increasingly controlled, limiting all risk. It is a natural consequence that limiting risk creates an often stale, uninspiring environment.

It is natural that today there is a genuine call for better leadership, broader vision, and a focus on building a business strategy that embraces environmental, economic, cultural, and social sustainability. The real question which should be posed is: why is it that such gulfs were allowed to develop and grow? Why is it that many resorts and hotels worked so independently of their communities?

One of the reasons is that there has been a preoccupation with business models over-the value of culture and people. It was driven by a change in the base business ethos over-the years. Russell Kett, Chairman of HVS, explained some of the reasoning for the change in leadership priorities:

> One of the fundamental changes is that leadership has moved from people who were traditionally hoteliers, who grew up having been to a hotel school, join a hotel company, worked their way up through the company, developed skills along the way, were seen to managers, then leaders and possessed a lot of hands on experience in operating hotels. Those are the leaders of yesterday. Today's leaders have a much greater focus on understanding the business itself, what drives the business, they may not even have worked within a hotel but they do have the ability to be able to lead a company, and know what to do when it comes to making improvement, when it is necessary to deliver an increased shareholder value and that is why leadership has evolved to where it is today.
>
> The reason for the change? I think the shareholders have increasingly required the leaders of hotel companies to deliver an increased return on investment. In doing so, they have taken the lead in requiring the companies to be better managed, better operated, better led, by people whose experiences are broader than

purely being greater hoteliers. The shareholders have dictated the change and the hotel sector has followed.

There has been an evolution of separating the bricks from the brains, traditionally the owner of the hotel would also operate. The management of the hotels have become more separated from the ownership of the actual assets and within the management, you have also got the split between the branding and the operation. The business model has evolved. Franchising has increased. Management companies have increased along with the ownership model having changed. You today have a focus on each component being optimised to be able to deliver a greater return in the investment. That is the driver. How can we make more money? It is a more sophisticated business model and it has been very successful.

As shareholders have asked for more, so it is natural that this demand has ripples and impacts the business models in different ways.

In the early 2000s, a very senior industry figure spoke in a seminar at the Ecole hoteliere de Lausanne, one of the world's leading hotel schools, and noted that for many of the FTSE 500 CEOs, the average lifespan was less than 5 years and therefore, they had little time to focus on people and culture. All that mattered, it was argued, was shareholder return and trying to maintain tenure. This always seemed to be a negative philosophy which was bound to create long-term problems. It was also a failure to fulfill the duties of a CEO as, like it or not, people and culture are part of the job. A leader has the power to select their priorities but it does have ramifications.

There is no doubt that the role of CEO has become increasingly harder as everyone has also had to learn new skills to go alongside the increased expectancies of recent times. We live in an era where the pace of change has been accelerating. Companies have been working to tighter margins, have been having to fight to retain relevance either among their target audiences, against their traditional competitors, or against new market entrants who are reshaping market dynamics. Given all this, it is no surprise that the average lifespan of an FTSE-listed company is decreasing.

Of the 100 companies in the FTSE 100 in 1984, only 24 were still breathing in 2012. The survival factor for today's companies relies on having an established leadership that can combine a working knowledge of the company or industry with the commercial acumen needed to operate in a globalized market experiencing a fast pace of change.

A Move Toward Localism

It is a strange irony that so much has been written about globalization and brands over-the last decade and yet, when Covid-19 has come calling, many have found greater joy and pleasure in localism and rediscovering communities, and of course, hospitality can play a key role as it sits in the heart of every community.

As more and more people look toward seeking something which is genuine and authentic, so they are turning to their local communities, its history, and its produce and culture. For some, the importance lies in their vineyards, their food, wine, and produce.

Hotels, resorts, restaurants, and bars can play a far more proactive role in telling the story of their community's history and cultural legacy. As guests seek ever greater experiences, it is a natural link for hospitality to be an ambassador for the culture of their region. *As localism becomes ever more important, so hospitality has a genuine opportunity to show its genuine modern importance in culture and society.* Hospitality can bring people together, bring a stable pillar that sits at the center of communities.

In so many ways, *it could be an exciting opportunity for those who grasp the opportunity.* It is nothing new, simply finding a renewed voice. When one travels across France and Italy, one expects to engage by the great wines and produce of the regions. The French have long argued that their gastronomy has always been the best in the world as each region has stayed true to its own regional recipes, passed down from generation rather than create new fusions and food styles. It is the same in Italy as Italians take great pride in their regional dishes and produce. It is genuine and authentic and one of the pleasures of traveling across Europe.

Localism is becoming ever more important to millennials and the younger generations who are seeking a greater sense of belonging than the drive toward globalization which has dominated the last 20 years. They are finding purpose and mission within the communities in which they live rather than in corporate concerns where they feel disengaged and lacking faith in the core objectives. It is a sad reflection on the last decade.

Everyone talks about the new norm and the forecasts are that the new norm will not be about globalization but about the importance of communities and localism. It will be based off a deeper belief in sustainability, in its broadest sense-environment, culture, and social as well as economic. *There is a growing call for a kinder society, greater collaboration, and care. Hospitality has a major role to play. The equation which seems to be coming together is:*

Localism—Collaboration—Community togetherness—Celebrating local produce

One of the most recent discussions to come to the fore is an increased call for all hospitality operations to work closer with local suppliers and farmers who will provide items which are naturally fresher and with fewer air miles than many other products supplied. More companies are today ensuring that they purchase from local farms and suppliers as this is being asked for by consumers. This is just one example, but it does illustrate a gulf which grew between localism and major operations. Of course, the reasoning lay in pricing, but research today indicates consumers are happier to pay more for fresher and local produce. Moreover, consumers want to witness a real active relationship between major operations and local suppliers and traders. It is a renewal of a relationship which did break down.

Back in 2008/09, many believed major errors had been made, that values had been eroded, and that a new narrative would come to the fore alongside most companies making a major correction to their approaches. However, in truth, this did not happen.

At the heart lies a strong financial debate. On the one hand, many will note that, following the crash, it was those in middle- and lower-income brackets who took the brunt of the fallout and that very few directors were affected. If one looks at the U.S. postcrash, the statistics were stark:

- 8.8 million jobs lost
- Unemployment spiked to 10 percent by October 2009
- 8 million homes foreclosed

- $19.2 trillion in household wealth lost
- Home price declines of 40 percent on average—even steeper in some cities
- S and P 500 declined 38.5 percent in 2008
- $7.4 trillion in stock wealth lost from 2008/09, or $66,200 per household, on average
- Employee-sponsored savings or retirement account balances declined 27 percent in 2008
- Delinquency rates for adjustable rate mortgages climbed to nearly 30 percent by 2010 (7)

Were lessons learnt? It certainly changed much in financial services with greater regulation and stricter policies. One would like to think that the narrative did change in business and society too, but little really changed as it should have done. One article at the time noted:

With stock prices plummeting, profits evaporating, and millions of workers worldwide joining the ranks of the unemployed, one might assume that the chief executives of the world's largest companies lost their jobs in dramatic numbers in 2008. But that was not the case. CEOs demonstrated remarkable recession resistance last year. Although CEO turnover rose slightly on a global basis, from 13.8 percent in 2007 to 14.4 percent in 2008, Booz and Company's annual survey reveals that turnover actually declined in North America and Europe, the regions hit first and hardest by the economic downturn. (8)

The *Telegraph* noted that 1.3 million lost their jobs in the United Kingdom (9). Business did rebuild after 2009; business processes became dominant and there did seem to be a genuine growth and ever greater demand for shareholder returns which in turn placed greater pressure on leadership teams. Certainly, margins became tighter and the hoped-for investment in human capital and in new innovation in sustainability just did not take place as was hoped.

The counter argument to the aforementioned was that real estate in many markets increased by over-three- to fourfold, creating mass speculation. So is a loss of a 40 percent against a gain of 300 percent really a loss? The same is true for stocks. Most were still higher than 5 years earlier.

It is a fair counter argument and does explain Russell Kett's perspective that:

> There has been an evolution of separating the bricks from the brains, traditionally the owner of the hotel would also operate. The management of the hotels have become more separated from the ownership of the actual assets and within the management, you have also got the split between the branding and the operation. The business model has evolved. Franchising has increased. Management companies have increased along with the ownership model having changed. You today have a focus on each component being optimised to be able to deliver a greater return in the investment. That is the driver. How can we make more money? It is a more sophisticated business model and it has been very successful.

The question therefore is: where is the balance to be found? Has this led to too much dominance of thinking of value at the expense of mission, values, and culture?

In a recent meeting, a number of leading financial experts excused themselves from a meeting to discuss "sustainability" as being a soft topic area. In their eyes, it may well be but how the issue is engaged may well determine future performance. The inevitable result was that the great change in narrative that had been so often talked about in 2009 never really happened. The focus was more on stability and economic recovery. Business models remained relatively stable and levels of investment into nonessential areas naturally fell. Maybe understandably so but it did serve to lay the ground for greater discontentment amongst emerging leaders in the ethics of business, arguably higher levels of disengagement, and an erosion of trust in leadership teams.

During the last decade, there has been a growing frustration that sustainability has not had the opportunity to make the progress that was so hoped for even back in the 1990s. It has been a slow move to become a central topic. But central it has become in company's strategies which have been driven by customers wanting to see a greater focus on social and environmental sustainability. Given the background, it is not hard to understand that the lack of any real change across the business sector, after the crash of 2008/09, could well prove to be the driving motivation and catalyst for change today. It is interesting that 2008/09 marked the start of the real concern over-the fall in average employee productivity and that this has been a major concern ever since. There is a logical argument to suggest a correlation between a lack of change in business models and in the narrative after such a crisis to a fall in trust in leadership, a fall in productivity, and a continuing tension between leaders and middle management who have felt under increased financial strain ever since. Add into this equation the fact that many graduates are emerging into the workplace with greater debt, feeling highly vulnerable, and wanting to see genuine change take place now.

This is a genuine problem area. Students in England are going to graduate with average debts of £50,800, after interest rates are raised on student loans to 6.1 percent, according to the Institute for Fiscal Studies. Those from the poorest backgrounds, with more loans available to support them, will graduate with debts of over £57,000 says the think tank. With the fallout from the Covid crisis, many feel economically vulnerable as they can only see getting on the housing ladder becoming harder and with a deep recession pending.

With the average house costing £231,855, according to the Office for National Statistics (ONS), borrowers who had banked on getting a mortgage with a 10 percent deposit would have put aside £23,185. However, it is being reported that many mortgage providers are asking for a 15 percent deposit so that the new owners do not face the prospect of negative equity if the recession is deep. This means, for a 15 percent deposit, they will now need to save an additional £11,600.

One of the great successes of the 1980s and 1990s lay in creating a belief in upward social mobility and the ability to generate wealth via home ownership. With increased levels of debt coupled with higher requirements for a mortgage, it is understandable that the young do feel that need to be given greater opportunities to be empowered and enabled to earn more. The call for greater progress in building sustainable business will grow louder and stronger. Investors today are looking far more closely at companies, also wanting to see real action in how leadership teams show progressive thinking in their behaviors toward their own people, the communities in which they operate, and the environment. Pressure today is building from both sides on leadership teams—from above with investors and from below from teams who ask to see better. It is only natural that change will now take place. It may have been change that should have taken place a decade ago. One could argue the point, but this change will grow now as the millennials begin to move into positions of authority and power.

Other factors may contribute to this change resulting in a radical change from the last decade. The Covid-19 crisis may be the catalyst in retrospect, but in truth, the ground was laid before the 2008/09 crash that just served to build the pressure in the system. The rise of a new generation will naturally see new values and philosophies emerge too. It is all part of a natural evolution.

The 2008/09 crash may have had a negative effect on developments in sustainability but the 2010s have seen a greater understanding of the challenges to be faced and what needs to be done. The challenge now in the 2020s is to ensure that real change does take place. There are no more excuses, no more space for delay. It is time for both environmental and social change.

CHAPTER 2

Sustainable Business

Business sustainability has come a long way in the last 50 years. It has been building a gradual momentum with each passing decade. The argument for sustainability really began in the 1970s with the establishment of environmental regulations. However, in those days it had a peripheral focus. Today, it has become central and a strategic concern which is beginning to influence markets, thinking, and behaviors.

In the research for this book, 100 leading Industry players were interviewed and 67 percent noted that sustainability played a central role in their strategies. Fifty-eight percent believed that hotels and restaurants play an important social role. Of course, one would hope that the percentages of both these issues were higher, ideally in the 80 percent levels, but it is progress. It has been a long road for those campaigning for greater focus on sustainability issues.

Of more concern were a number of other results which emerged:

- One of the most striking features is that the results high-lighted some of the "battlegrounds" in terms of people issues, most especially with regard to diversity, inclusion, and welfare.
  - Only 34 percent believed that mental health, stress, and anxiety had become an issue of concern and 41 percent disagreed that this was a key area. Given that it has been well documented that 1:4 today will suffer from a mental health issue during their careers, it is clear that there is still a need for greater understanding. There is much research which indicates that the increased financial strains placed on middle- and lower-level income employees is at the heart of the increased anxiety and stress. One makes a strong argument that their business models have been pushed to their boundaries in order to achieve maximum

results, rewarding the most senior players but placing strain
on the lower levels.

The 2019 Vitality "Healthiest Companies" research would support such an argument (10). It stated:

(a) Overall, the results suggest that the employees who took part
in the survey lost 14.6 percent of their working hours due to
absence (1.1 percent), and presenteeism (13.4 percent).

(b) This represents a loss of 38 productive days per employee
per year.

(c) Lower income employees are the most at-risk for mental
health issues, with 16.4 percent of those earning less than
£20,000 indicating that they suffer from depression.

(d) Financial concerns are very common, with 51.1 percent of
employees reporting at least some level of concern.

Other results from the research, conducted for this book, with the
100 senior players noted that:

- Only 61 percent indicated that diverse teams were of real
  importance.
- 38 percent noted that emerging talent had not been helped by
  a reduced focus on talent development programs.
- It is interesting that 62 percent accepted that there has been
  an increased lack of trust in leaders and at the same time,
  67 percent believed that leaders should be more visible, with
  78 percent accepting that leaders had become less visible.
- On the positive, sustainability has clearly become a core area
  today for all businesses. It has moved from a periphery issue
  to core over the last decade and now seems well accepted.
- It is also encouraging that 58 percent believed that hotels do
  have a key social role to play within their communities.
- It is also interesting to note that 64 percent believed that
  customers today are seeking enhanced customer experiences.

One can read many articles and reports that display a deep level of
frustration at the progress in both environmental and social programs,

often left frustrated by business leaders and politicians who have had their eye too firmly focused on GDP, revenues, and economics. It has created a tense battleground. As noted in Chapter 1, real change was poised to take place a decade ago, but the 2008/09 crash did "delay" progress. However, the emergence of new generations who are customers and who do place the environment and society first is creating a natural process of change. There is a general awareness today that all companies need to possess both environmental and social strategies. It is simply unacceptable for this not to exist and this is a long way from where the minds of leaders lay a decade ago. Abigail Tan, CEO of the St. Giles Group of Hotels, noted:

> It is very important to display what we are doing in order to reduce our carbon footprint and impact on the environment, and to create sustainable business, hotels, and environments. Environments also include our internal teams that need to be able to grow and be sustainable as a culture and family.
>
> We developed a campaign called #CitizenG–United to being Globally Green to launch a sustainability drive and push for our hotels to continue the journey and to attempt to be at the forefront of sustainable buildings and environments.

Abigail Tan's comment is a sign of a new narrative emerging, with an increased focus not only on environmental impact but also on the internal importance of teams, people, and culture

In August 2020, a new hotel was launched—The Birch Hotel, in Hertfordshire, England. The hotel reflects the new thinking which is beginning to emerge. It is a resort based in 55 acres and includes a farm, a bakery, a potter studio, art studio, and wellness studios. It has a clear focus on social interaction, on being an escape from urban living and on community. It even has a website entitled: https://birchcommunity.com

The hotel brings together a strong sustainability theme but combined with health and wellness and the need to reconnect with the natural environment. It is an exciting new development which does mark a new thinking emerging within hospitality. One of the cofounders, Chris Penn, talks about his aim to create a new "experience" for the guest sitting at the heart of the ethos.

Progress is being made and it is growing with time. In the noughties, it was a campaign for change; today it has become an inevitability and its relevance in writing about it lies in the fact that future leaders will need to think not just about the business they lead, but also about society and environment. Leadership is changing as it is becoming far more multidimensional and complex. In past times, business leaders were judged by the performance of their business. Today's leaders need to be far more broad-minded in their thinking and approach. One can make a strong argument that the leadership styles that dominated thinking at the time of the 2008/09 crash would no longer be viewed as correct or acceptable today; that is how far change has happened in the last decade.

There is a genuine momentum of change taking place across most companies today. More and more companies are openly declaring that sustainability is important to their company's success. Companies are developing sustainability strategies, marketing sustainable products and services, creating positions such as chief sustainability officer, and publishing sustainability reports for consumers, investors, pressure groups, and the public at large. New words are being created, along with new definitions and a new understanding. The new thinkings displayed by both the Birch Hotel and by Abigail Tan are examples. Both are millennial leaders emerging to lead through a new narrative which does have a bigger aspiration at its heart.

Research indicates that over 88 percent of business school students think that learning about social and environmental issues in business is a priority (11). Sixty-seven percent want to incorporate environmental sustainability into their future jobs (12). This does illustrate the high level of change taking place across the generations and their values.

It is also telling that Stanford University notes that the percentage of business schools that require students to take a course dedicated to business and society increased from 34 percent in 2001 to 79 percent in 2011, and specific academic programs on business sustainability can now be found in 46 percent of the top 100 U.S. master of business administration (MBA) programs (13).

The question is fairly posed that, as knowledge and awareness in sustainability has increased, why is it then that problems such as climate change, water scarcity, and species extinction have continued to worsen?

A fair question, but the answer lies in the traditional priorities of leaders, in economics, and in the need for real pressure and desire for change to emerge with new generations. As noted, sustainability has been the victim of the long battleground between business, economic, and environmental needs. It is a natural area of tension. How does one marry GDP growth, increased economic prosperity, alongside the need to create genuine environmental change?

There has been a misperception that having a strong sustainability concept requires investment and is more expensive than traditional approaches. However, environmental technology can be more cost effective and more long-lasting and so, there is a strong argument to support investment in new technologies. As an example, renewable energy, also known as "clean energy," is energy that is collected from renewable resources which are naturally replenished such as sunlight, wind, rain, tides, waves, and geothermal heat. Modern environmental technology has enabled us to capture this naturally occurring energy and convert it into electricity or useful heat through devices such as solar panels and wind and water turbines, which reflect a highly positive impact of technology on the environment.

Having overtaken coal in 2015 to become the second largest generator of electricity, renewable sources currently produce more than 20 percent of the United Kingdom's electricity, and EU targets mean that this is likely to increase to 30 percent by 2020. While many renewable energy projects are large scale, renewable technologies are also suited to remote areas and developing countries, where energy is often crucial in human development.

The cost of renewable energy technologies such as solar panels and wind turbines is falling, and government investment is on the rise. This has contributed toward the amount of rooftop solar installations in Australia growing from approximately 4,600 households to over 1.6 million between 2007 and 2017.

It takes time to change mindsets. It takes time to argue the case for what is often seen as medium- to long-term investment but gradually the case is being made and growing in its strength.

The concept of "sustainable business" is building momentum and more investors as well as emerging generations want to see greater action in this area. New products and new services are emerging all the time, and this will create a further momentum for change.

Perhaps one such illustration has been on the modern theme of "a caring economy," which many believe is emerging. The argument is that the Covid-19 crisis will be seen as a catalyst for genuine change in the call for sustainable business as it has also seen an increased call for care, courage, and kindness. The crisis has given all a chance to stop, and reflect. One company recently (June 2020) researched their employees and discovered that over 65 percent of their employees had no desire to return to the office. Interestingly feedback also told them that many felt they were more productive working from home as they were in safe spaces, with no distractions and no "office politics" to impact on performance. Further feedback also indicated that one of the core reasons that many wanted to work from home is that they found greater "joy and meaning" with greater interaction with their local communities. The whole concept of community has become a dominant theme during 2020.

It is one of the great unknowns at this time but there is little doubt that many have felt inspired by great examples of care such as the singing heard on the Italian balconies during their lockdown period, to various examples of songs being recreated by teams in companies, brought together by music. By the way, many hospitality companies have come to the fore to combat food poverty.

There are many companies who are already planning to continue some of the great works that they began during the Covid-19 crisis as they have seen firsthand how it has helped bring teams together, seen the pride in behaviors return back into their companies. There is a strong and clearer link today between social and business sustainability. The two can very much work hand in hand in a way that has not been achieved in the past 20 years. If one returns to the base principles of how both the U.S. and U.K. economies did rebuild after World War II, it was a mix of more experienced and skilled officers returning from war, combined with a greater sense of compassion and care for others. Business planning did return to the basics and ensured that there were firm pillars from which to rebuild. Leaders understood they played a major role both in the life of the business and in the lives of their employees and their families. In return, employees were loyal to their employers and many would spend their whole career with one company. Why? At the heart there was a belief in community which became gradually eroded with time and new management philosophies.

The counter argument, of course, is that hard economics and the need to rebuild economies will see behaviors revert to previous norms. To a level this will certainly be true, but the trend existed precrisis and suggests that the movement in achieving greater social and business sustainability is unlikely to be halted.

In fairness to the U.K. government, they stepped forward and won much praise with their Furlough scheme which did not just protect 11 million jobs, but also freed up many to be able to volunteer and play important social roles. There are major problems to be solved and it will take many years to solve but the indications are good.

Will real change emerge from the Covid-19 crisis? It can be debated but it is unlikely to be just because of the crisis. Just as the concept of sustainable business calls for a long-term strategy, so too does the process of change need to be viewed through a long-term lens. The real change will take place as new generations emerge with new ideologies.

Progress is being made but the argument for change needs to be thoroughly reasoned, with considered viewpoints. It is a time for serious people, serious leadership through genuine, authentic actions and words. People want to trust in leadership again. They need to. Leadership does have a major role to play across all societies and for too long trust in leadership has been eroding. Leadership has long sat at the heart of most cultures. As the pace of change is so fast today, it is important to share knowledge and ideas in a far more proactive fashion than has been needed to be the case before. As the world has become more open, more transparent, so leadership has had to change in many ways. It has been on its own journey during the digital age. It has not always been an easy journey as many have grasped the advancements of the new age and not always understood its ramifications. There has been a growing cry for change and a stronger balance to be found in business between wealth creation, talent, and sustainability.

The need is for stronger business arguments to be made as this then inspires change. Real change is often seen through generational change and in response to major crises. Both are happening at this time and new emerging technology is making the argument fundamentally stronger. It is interesting that the Covid crisis has seen many companies look to embrace new digital technology such as apps which allow customers to be able to access stronger service levels from companies.

Signs of genuine market transformation are beginning to happen. This is being naturally driven by market forces: the demands of the emerging generations and the increased interest of investors in sustainability progress.

During 2019 and early 2020, there has been a growing understanding that if a company wants to attract the best people and talent, then they need to act and operate in a stronger, more socially aware and sustainable manner. Rather than threaten results, it arguably makes a company more competitive. Leaders have been forced to start to think more broadly as market dynamics have demanded so.

On this basis, many companies started to create strategies which focused on their becoming increasingly economically, environmentally, and socially responsible—and in turn creating a more sustainable business model.

There was a very strong business case for the change:

- Global sustainable investment is up 10-fold since 2004 and stands in 2020 at US$30 trillion.
- Marketplace dynamics have been changing as have regulations and societal demand.
- Sustainability today impacts on relationships with investors, shareholders, the communities in which companies are based, and the people that are employees.
- Generational shift—the leading young talent will join those companies that possess values and beliefs that are aligned to their own.

Interestingly, prior to the pandemic, more companies had already begun to implement new ideas. The financial sector took the brunt of the criticism following the 2008/09 crash, but they are also the ones who seem to be leading the development of new and improved philosophies. Critics argue they have needed to do this to both be able to attract the best talent, which today wants to work for those who are committed to a broader agenda, and to rebuild lost trust in the system. It has been a decade and a long journey for many and still the perception is poor. Earlier in this book, a senior player from the financial sector was quoted as saying:

> One of the biggest shifts has been an understanding that we were consistently losing respect because we were seen to be untrustworthy. Of course, this meant that we would lose clients and not be able to attract the best talent that we wanted. It was a hard realisation. It did remind me of the Conservative Party back in about 2002 when they openly accepted that they were seen as "The Nasty Party". It took them five years to accept and another seven or eight years to become electable. It has probably taken us a decade to accept and it may take another decade to win back real trust but that is the journey we have to begin.

Often cultures do lose their way and it does take time for an acceptance that things are wrong to be accepted. It was former Prime Minister Theresa May who, in 2002, surprised her own party's conference with a description that the party had become to be "The Nasty Party." The term was used to explain two election defeats and for the party being often seen as nonprogressive, antigay, antiminorities, probusiness, and lacking concern for the poor.

The former Conservative Government, under John Major, between 1992 and 1997 has seen a whole series of scandals which undermined the good work that it did with the economy. It simply lost trust, an emotion that Tony Blair tapped into to win a landslide in 1997. Blair's rise to government led to a genuine belief that politics would change, that they would stand for higher behaviors and standards. It gave Blair a momentum to win two elections but also explains the disappointment of many with the argument for war in Iraq which was to follow in 2002/03.

Of course, one can argue these points, but the most important point is that the financial sector is leading a genuine change which will make others want to follow.

Support of the Community as a Path
to Leadership Growth

Most organizations donate financially to any number of worthy causes. Sometimes these causes align with their core business. Food companies often address hunger charities and the Covid crisis showed how many causes really came to the fore to help the vulnerable. Many of the leading financial institutions have started to be actively involved within their communities as it attracts the best talent who wants to be involved with companies who do contribute and also changes the poor image that many had after the crash of 2008/09 and during the austerity era. However, by 2020, donations alone are not seen to be enough. There has been a growing cynicism that many companies take the praise for a simple donation which is then written off against tax. Where is the real intent? The real action?

It needs to be far more than just a donation of funds. It needs to be active and meaningful involvement. There is nothing wrong with donations, but it does not create an emotional connection between employees and the cause. There has also been a growing cynicism which has emerged over those companies which donate simply to enable a box-ticking exercise to say that they have donated, rather than actually caring about a cause.

This was already changing, and companies are now investing into key projects for the reasons outlined earlier. Companies have realized that it is no longer good enough to present their CSR programs and outline a number of areas where their donations are impacting around the world. In 2020, the demand is for far better. Audiences—employees, clients, consumers, and investors—are wanting to know whether the company does walk its own talk. Does it really believe in the work that it is investing in or is it just lip service?

It has been fascinating to observe how the City of London's landscape has changed in many subtle ways: the number of gardens of the roofs of major corporations, the number of beehives also being placed in appropriate location on roofs, and even how buildings are being designed today with the most modern techniques to maximize and support sustainable technology.

The Coronavirus has taken this to another level as it highlighted the plight of the vulnerable all across society and the globe. Companies have stepped forward to invest in help. Many employees found themselves volunteering for causes which they believed in and CEOs found that their people found a real sense of pride and purpose in how they and their companies were behaving in a time of crisis. Many leaders started to talk more openly of their own role in investing back into communities. Companies today are crossing old forbidden lines as they now want to play an active role in their communities and their people.

A Renewal of Leadership as Service for Others Before Self

Service leadership is, first and foremost, about putting aside personal concerns to prioritize the needs of others. It is what has long marked out hospitality, a desire to serve others and bring pleasure and comfort to guests. The desire to serve others is something which is often a "calling." Leading hospitality professionals are often motivated by a desire to create safety, pleasure, and an experience for guests. They want to create a home away from home for their guests. Service leadership has been the heart of hospitality over many centuries.

One can argue that the "service ethos" has been challenged in hospitality over the last 25 years as many began to see hotels as retail operations with rooms, as almost a perishable good. This focus increased with the advancement in the Internet and, of course, the ability to adapt pricing during the course of the day, week, or month. This has become an important skill within hospitality and has helped to maximize potential. However, hospitality is all about a delicate balance between new skills to engage custom along with the provision of a service. Hospitality needs this balance and is coming back into vogue as customers are seeking both greater experiences and greater breadth in diets and offer to be made available. Services have had to evolve and adapt just as leadership will need to change to embrace the new demands of both customers and employees.

Politics too has long been about public service. In past times, some would enter politics once they had had a successful career in business. However, over the years many became career politicians, starting from a young age. This created an erosion in the concept of public service as it was felt too many politicians were focused primarily on their own gain. Leadership should always be more than just about one's self. It needs to be about those that a leader represents and not just the shareholders or voters, although clearly this is a primary group that will determine a leader's tenure. It should importantly also be about employees and clients/customers. During the Covid-19 crisis, many companies stripped back their strategies and returned to core values: the "why" for the existing business. They understood that today's demand is for the genuine and authentic message and every company needed to have a clear mission that their clients would understand and, importantly, trust.

Change Is Taking Place Step by Step

Critics on progress argue that there is still a lot of work to be achieved in order to correct many of the major environmental, social, and cultural issues which do still exist. They are correct: there is much to be done. Another argument is that it is only in the last five years that the issue has been taken seriously and then the question is, is this too late?

Culture within a company used to be a major talking point. Over the last 10 years, culture has hardly been mentioned and has almost become a luxury. Thirty years ago, the culture of a company was viewed to be almost the secret "x" factor which would drive performance and productivity. The focus on culture arguably became lost as companies focused more on business process, models, and technology. These became the secret drivers and measures for business performance. There are many who argue that investment in culture declined the more that venture capitalists became involved in business. Their focus, understandably, was to create greater wealth which in turn improved pensions, but at what cost? Should business possess a broader role to play than just wealth creation? This is one of the most important discussion pieces taking place today. Is it possible that the lack of investment in a company's culture and mission serves to also accidently undermine the engagement and loyalty of employees? Even of productivity? In order to maximize performance, does a company need to possess a strong mission and purpose?

It is important to note at this point that there is a genuine difference between mission and mission statement. Many became cynical about the mission statements that companies produced which would invariably declare a desire to be an excellent employer and be world class. A mission is more fundamental. It defines the genuine purpose for why the business exists. What is its reason for existing?

Companies have certainly become more efficient and controlled business, but at what cost? One school of thought will argue that business has never been better controlled. A counter is that productivity and employee engagement have never been worse. How does one find the right balance?

To describe the point, the author began his career in hospitality in a management role for a country hotel. Each week the trading figures would be filled in by hand and posted to the central accounts office. If there was a problem, then there were three to four days before the problem would be picked up which would allow time for a solution to be found. There are two points to be considered with this. For the company, this margin of error also means there is potential risk in play. Greater controls mitigated that risk and took the responsibility for problem solving away from the manager. For the manager, the learning was better for working to solve the problem and to have the freedom, the empowerment to solve the problem. By mitigating risk through control, the company also hindered the best learning.

One of the most common discussions today is that it is well documented that many emerging talents are fearful of taking risk, of failure. However, this is an important tool in learning and growth. The more a company wishes to limit the risk, the more it also limits the potential to enable talent and encourage risk taking.

What do you believe is the right balance to be found?

It certainly has been a long journey and the challenge for the decade ahead is now to create genuine and lasting change. The past year has also seen a wave of grassroots protests around the world against climate inaction, including those initiated by Extinction Rebellion activists and hundreds of thousands of students inspired by the Swedish teenager Greta Thunberg's "striking for climate." Whatever one's views of such a young voice leading the campaign for change, there is no doubting that she has made an immense impact.

The argument is that the world's future consumers and voters are increasingly intolerant of failure to tackle climate change and social justice issues. Business and investors have started to create processes and actions which could be very influential for their future prospects.

As previously noted, it is no accident that the major leaders in change are financial services companies, investors, insurers, and lenders who do often possess the vision when it comes to acknowledging where the risks of failing to deal with sustainability issues lie. The year 2020 may be a moment where old economics and the modern world's aspirations come together and this hopefully will create the landscape for the future actions to come. Instead of waiting for a market shift to create incentives for sustainable practices, companies are creating those shifts to enable new forms of business sustainability.

Perhaps for the first time, companies are beginning to see opportunity, not just threat and risk. Renewable energy and associated technologies such as electric vehicles are becoming cheaper and more competitive, making it easier for companies to make the sustainable choice. This too has been important.

It is true that still relatively few companies have committed to these initiatives; those that have are among the biggest corporations in the world, and their efforts to meet their own targets will encourage their suppliers to become more sustainable in turn.

The drivers for companies to become more sustainable are coming from many directions and growing exponentially: from the science, initiatives from governments and regulators, increased consumer pressure, and demands from investors. The best prepared businesses see opportunities as well as risks and are preparing accordingly.

As has been noted, real change can only be generated with supporting economic arguments. If sustainability advancement can change the way that business acts and behaves then this creates a greater education as more business leaders listen. Economics is still the hard truth which will influence the most. Until the economic argument is won, change at any great level will not take place and this argument today is being made and won. It is the game changer. Business today is global and so it can influence on a global scale far better and more impactfully than politics.

Hospitality can play a very important role as hotels do sit at the heart of every community around the world and it can highlight a commitment to sustainability. Martin Rinck, Global Head of Luxury and Lifestyle brand with Hilton, commented:

> The importance of sustainability cannot be emphasised enough. It is the way of the future. Customers want to know that the brand that they are associating themselves with does contribute to the benefit of society. Alternatively, they will avoid brands that do not deploy sustainable practices or that are careless with the environment. Conrad Hotels and Resorts, in particular, is a brand that is grounded on impact, making an impact on the world through sustainable practices and through the preservation of art, history, culture. The parent company for the Conrad brand, Hilton, is as a company incredibly committed to redefining sustainable travel through their "Travel with purpose programme".
>
> Over-a decade ago, Hilton became the first major hotel brand to make sustainability a brand standard. We required all of our hotels globally to measure and manage their environmental performance through our award winning, cloud based corporate responsibility management system.
>
> In 2018, we launched our ambitious "travel with purpose" programme. By 2030, our goal is to cut our environmental footprint by 50% and double our investment in social impact. As part of the 2030 goals, we are the first major hotel company to institute science-based targets to reduce our carbon emissions and commit to zero soap to landfills.

It is a strong commitment but more importantly is an example of the narrative that many hoped would emerge post-2008/09. Martin Rinck's (Global Head of Luxury and Lifestyle brand) argument is that it did emerge post-2008/09, but in 2010 was still a narrative of the few. Today, it is slowly becoming the narrative of the majority and that will create the change needed.

Social Sustainability

The other key area of discussion and debate for business has naturally been about social responsibility. This is a key pillar in any business strategy on sustainability.

Social sustainability is about identifying and managing business impacts, both positive and negative, on people and on communities. Social sustainability has been too often overlooked during the past 20 years: the effect that a company has on communities via its employees and on local business. Too often businesses were viewed as stand-alone entities, separate from their communities, but this too is beginning to see a new narrative emerge.

In any genuine social strategy:

- Business should understand their role in improving the lives of the people they employ and interact with. This can be through employment, trade, or creating a destination which positively impacts on the community as a whole.
  - Hotels and restaurants have major roles to play as they can be destinations in their own right. Hotels talk often to a global audience and can therefore represent the culture and story of the local community almost better than anything else. Hotels really do have a major social role to play. The hotel sector has often felt that it has not been as well respected or valued as it could be. Strangely enough, this perception has often been more internal than external. Many have long admired great hotels and restaurants, although acknowledging the natural risks connected with being an investor. However, hotels and restaurants can play an important role in bringing people together, in being the center of communities and, even more, telling the stories of those communities.
- Businesses should consider strategic social investments and promote social initiatives that impact positively on the local community.
- Partner with other local businesses, bringing together united strengths to make a greater positive impact.

One of the questions frequently asked is whether many resorts and major hotels have understood the real role that they can play in representing the historical story and culture of a community. Today's travellers and customers are looking for something deeper, more genuine, authentic experiences that do connect them to the culture and community that they are visiting. Hotels can be the stage that can tell the story and attract local customs which in turn, of course, supports the economics of many local communities.

All businesses today have a major role to play in the communities in which they operate and can play a public service role which has arguably been missing through politics.

The Balance Between Culture and Business Models

It is a very fragile relationship and, as has been indicated previously, is one that arguably has not been invested in or worked on hard enough. There has been, in recent years, a preoccupation with business models over the value of culture and people. This was driven by a change in business ethos. Russell Kett, Chairman of HVS, explained some of the reasoning for the change in leadership priorities:

> One of the fundamental changes is that leadership has moved from people who were traditionally hoteliers, who grew up having been to a hotel school, joined a hotel company, worked their way up through the company, developed skills along the way, were seen to be managers, then leaders and possessed a lot of hands on experience in operating hotels. Those are the leaders of yesterday. Today's leaders have a much greater focus on understanding the business itself, what drives the business, they may not even have worked within a hotel but they do have the ability to be able to lead a company, and know what to do when it comes to making improvements, when it is necessary to deliver an increased shareholder value and that is why leadership has evolved to where it is today.
>
> The reason for the change? I think the shareholders have increasingly required the leaders of hotel companies to deliver an increased return on investment. In doing so, they have taken

the lead in requiring the companies to be better managed, better operated, better led, by people whose experiences are broader than purely being greater hoteliers. The shareholders have dictated the change and the hotel sector has followed.

As shareholders have asked for more, so it is natural that this demand has rippled and impacted business models in different ways.

In the early 2000s, a very senior industry figure spoke at a seminar at the Ecole hôtelière de Lausanne (14), one of the World's leading hotel schools, and noted that for many of the FTSE 500 CEOs, the average lifespan was less than five years' tenure in role and therefore, they had little time to focus on people and culture. The primary focus, it was argued, had to be on shareholder return and trying to maintain tenure. Only by achieving this could one maintain stability and consistency in leadership. This always seemed to be both a negative philosophy and one which was bound to create long-term problems. The question to be considered is: can a leader choose not to invest in people and culture just because it may impact directly on shareholder value? Technically they clearly have the right but, morally, isn't the duty of a CEO to ensure that employees are developed, trained, and invested in too? Leaders have the power to select their priorities, but it does have ramifications.

There is no doubt that the role of CEO has become increasingly harder as everyone has also had to learn new skills to go alongside the increased expectancies of recent times. We live in an era where the pace of change has been accelerating. Companies have been working to tighter margins, have been fighting to retain relevance either among their target audiences, against their traditional competitors, or against new market entrants who are reshaping market dynamics. Given all this, it is no surprise that the average lifespan of an FTSE-listed company is decreasing. One can argue that this has always been the case, so what is new? There has been a gradual erosion in any real business thinking around its impact on communities, on society, on environment, and on people. Business thinking became ever more narrow over the years and this was made even more so with the advancement in technology. A focus on sustainable business is also a focus on having strong pillars to support that business over the long term.

Of the 100 companies in the FTSE 100 in 1984, only 24 were still breathing in 2012 (15). The survival factor for today's companies relies on having an established leadership that can combine a working knowledge of the company or industry with the commercial acumen needed to operate in a globalized market experiencing a fast pace of change.

Interestingly, just as the pace of change continues to accelerate so we are now seeing the emergence of a greater variety of industry/discipline backgrounds among the top FTSE leaders. It used to be an understanding that most CEOs would have a financial background, but this is now changing and a growing percentage have a technology or digital background as companies seek to compete via new methodologies. An increasing number of CEOs are from marketing background and even from HR. Companies can simply not afford to keep still. Organizations are grasping at the opportunities digital transformation presents and need leaders that can embrace this mindset and use it to create new growth opportunities or protect competitive advantage. Hospitality is the industry that sits almost with old-fashioned values and beliefs but is competing in a new space. It is no surprise therefore that new conflicts are emerging.

> Hotels and restaurants business modules have evolved, and the financial expectations have changed dramatically to be able to survive a more demanding market. Leaders have been forced to change. They have had to create new leadership styles to cope with the modern responsibilities of running a business. From the back seat to the front seat, leaders needed to be more involved with their business, to be more hands on and to be able to continually change and adapt to the markets…business modules are required to be far more dynamic, lighter and able to adapt within a shorter window of time to still achieve sustainable results. Cash flow was made the King of the business and the long-term cash investments were put to sleep.
>
> —Thomas Sorcinelli, Director of F and B at Heckfield Place

Russell Kett, Chairman of HVS, also underlined how the overall models and thinking have changed over the years:

There has been an evolution of separating the bricks from the brains, traditionally the owner of the hotel would also operate. The management of the hotels have become more separated from the ownership of the actual assets and within the management, you have also got the split between the branding and the operation. The business model has evolved. Franchising has increased. Management companies have increased along with the ownership model having changed. You today have a focus on each component being optimised to be able to deliver a greater return on the investment. That is the driver. How can we make more money? It is a more sophisticated business model and it has been very successful.

Should Leadership Boards Change in Structure?

With all the statistics which have been outlined, it is clear that there is a gulf between the traditional methodologies and the philosophies which sit at the heart of millennials. It is easy to see how many times both media and political commenters have been inaccurate in recent years. Their understanding has been based on the tradition and they have misunderstood how often external audiences have disengaged from their messages.

It is, in truth, the same within companies when leadership teams are still following a traditional doctrine with little true understanding that their messages and processes simply do not engage. As one understands this point, it is easy to then understand why there is such a chasm between the generations. The reported levels of disengagement have been ignored time and again. Little has been done to understand the social changes which have taken place. Thinking has too often been narrow with not enough understanding of how history and environment have influenced each passing generation of people and business.

One needs to remember that the Baby Boomers grew up in different times. In the 1970s respect for one's senior was central within work and social culture. Leadership was far more dictatorial, and the word of the leader was deemed as final. That is simply no longer the case with a modern society which will question everything. The processes and approaches of old no longer work. Leadership teams do need to adapt their thinking and approaches for the new generation which is emerging. The only place to start is with stronger engagement and the building of greater trust.

Many will argue that the starting place for change begins at board level as, at times, these have been less than properly functional. There is certainly evidence that many boards have been less than united in objective. This is natural as the pressure on a board would only have increased as the chasm developed between generations. The task is now to come together and be more effective if culture is to be strong and trust rebuilt. Where does that process start?

In simple terms this starts in four areas:

1. There does need to be far greater understanding of how to engage internal teams and audiences.
2. There does need to be a genuine desire for trust to be rebuilt.
3. The issue is that often the role of leader has attracted the wrong personalities in recent times: those focused on achieving results at all costs. Of course, this is an oversimplification but there has been a clear erosion of internal values and trust.
4. Companies need to possess a greater sense of mission and purpose based off strong values.

In simple terms, boards cannot be united if the leaders themselves do not embrace a wide agenda that works for all. In recent years many have been critical of HR but back in the 1970s and 1980s, HR operated to a far wider remit. As a result, they could have and did have a far more positive role to play on business. As business thinking became increasingly narrow and controlled, so HR's remit too became more limited and it became increasingly effective. One senior executive once noted that:

> HR changed role over the years. It used to be the central attacker with a focus on maximising the human asset. Then as more and more employment cases came to the fore, HR became the central defender with a role to defend the employer from risk. I know of many HR Directors who pride themselves on the decline in employment tribunal cases rather than the development of the

people and culture. It is not their fault. The world became legalistic and it impacted on risk and models.

At this time, there are many MDs (managing directors) and CEOs who are working with their teams on plans for how the business landscape may look as the world re-emerges from the Coronavirus lockdown and how services may change in emphasis. It could well be that this period/challenge offers an excellent opportunity for boards to come together as they have not done in recent times.

There has been a lot of debate over whether board structures have been truly effective in recent times as there has been an ever-growing balancing act between the demands of shareholders, asset managers, clients, customers, and employees. All this has been sitting on the shoulders of the CEOs or MDs whilst there has been a growing chasm as CMOs (chief marketing officers), HRDs (human resources directors), and CFOs (chief financial officers) who have created greater walls around their remits and are separated sometimes from these daily issues.

> I do smile as Marketing Directors sometimes talk to me in their language, which at times makes no sense and they look at me in a way that suggests that I should understand and maybe I am thick if I don't. If I handed them a P and L to manage, I suspect the colour would drain from their faces. Leadership is about doing, not talking; it is about what happens between our team and the customer. What is the relationship and is it a good one?
> —Adam Elliott, Founder, Paragon Hospitality

We have written about the lack of trust in leadership teams in recent times, but this does not all sit with the CEO/MD. It is also targeted at the other disciplines. Many have noted that they distrust the internal communications from their own marketing teams.

HR has become a well-debated battleground. The relationship between CEO and HR has not always been as healthy as it could be. Many in HR are fully aware that their roles have changed over the years and that there are those who do not view them in a positive light. There was a report that came out precrisis that noted that the majority of HRDs questioned the competence of their CEOs and were frustrated over how their budgets were viewed as a luxury.

Even if one is cynical over these results, there is little doubting the consistent research that has noted that leadership teams are distrusted by their own talent and research, noting the high level of stress across all levels. If there are such high levels of stress across all organizations, it must suggest that existing structures are not effective enough and that there is a need for change.

Many talk about structure and process; yet this seems to only apply to almost improving controls, purchasing, payments, job boards, and applications, which is fair enough but there is also a direct correlation between improved controls and erosion in trust. There is a clearly missing part of the jigsaw.

Most will accept that the pressure on businesses to deliver strong results has intensified but structures have remained remarkably similar over many years. Maybe is there a need for change? A change that brings together CMOs, HRDs, and CFOs to work together on strategic development to support the work on the CEOs/MDs who are shouldering much of the day-to-day pressures. To be provocative, perhaps CMOs and HRDs need to work closer together to ensure that messaging and communications are far more effective and progressive in how they reach out to internal and external audiences, across all diverse groups, all minorities, and all audiences.

There is a global tech product which was created to be a "best in class" platform for internal communications. Given all the issues and statistics noted, there is little doubt that this is a very important tool which should be an asset to many companies. Yet despite this they have found their average sale cycle is a one-year process as boards have simply not placed internal communication as a priority but rather as a luxury expense. There is endless research that will indicate that the cost of losing a middle manager can equate to between 2x and 5x of their annual salary in order to replace when one takes into account all costs from recruitment to lost customers to less productivity in the initial months. This can logically equate therefore to between $150,000 and $375,000. One only needs to retain one extra person to cover the cost and yet middle managers are seeking to leave at alarming levels.

There is a genuine need for a change in psychology at board level: one which places a bigger picture and objective before a narrow objective and remit. Trust needs to start at the board table and if this is a struggle, then perhaps that structure does need to change.

Whether one agrees with this or not, the bottom line is that each company is going to have to adjust its strategy to make sure it is competitive and that is going to take all disciplines working together as one. Trust will need to be of a far higher level than it has been, and this does need to start with the leadership team.

Business has become more pressured and it needs to adapt to new processes to ensure that it can meet the challenge. Boards of the late 1980s and early 1990s were far more united than one finds today. This may well be because the pressures and expectations were less but then there is even more reason for a need for boards to change.

Companies Are Thinking Too Narrowly So Why Not Bring in Fresh Thinking and Talent to Challenge Thoughts?

In late 2016, the Bank of England accepted that some of its forecasts post the Brexit vote have been inaccurate as they had themselves been too narrow in their thinking (16).

The argument is that there is a need for a greater breadth in how many boards think and act. Is there therefore an argument for bringing fresh talent in? Does the role of both chairman and the NEDs (nonexecutive director) need to be tougher in their structure so that this group does hold boards far better to account? This is not about challenging competence but ensuring that leadership teams are challenged to a higher level so that the right decisions are made.

Many who watch the House of Commons from afar will note that it sometimes looks like a playhouse of immature adolescents all screaming at each other. There is a fair argument to this but where the House of Commons (17) is so effective is that it is a small chamber that holds 650 members and this creates an often fierce "arena" that will hold leaders to account both verbally and physically. It can be an intimidating debating chamber where only the highly skilled will survive. It may appear to be a bit like a schoolyard, but it is brutally effective. No prime minister would want to face 250 to 300 opponents all standing within 100 ft. without the facts.

Being held to account is an important pillar in democracy and anyone who enters this arena needs to have a full grasp of the facts. It is, of course, understandable that a company will want to recruit an expert from their own sector and discipline. This has long been the case and argument. However, there is also a strong argument for bringing in fresh perspectives that can be married with the existing expertise within a company.

There are many exceptional talents seeking to break away from their own existing marketplaces to find fresh challenges in new sectors. There are genuine barriers to this taking place, although in truth it can be of real value to bring into a business a voice and intellect that will challenge the accepted norm. In a recent survey, it was noted that the majority believed that the thinking within their own business was often too narrow. This will not change unless those same companies are prepared to think more widely themselves. Why should their own teams think more broadly if the leadership teams still think the same way themselves?

It is argued today that with the advances in AI everyone will need to reinvent themselves as they progress through their careers. As the world evolves, so executives and all businesses need to change. Earlier, it was written that a CEO's tenure for an FTSE 100 company was less than five years. What happens to a CEO after their career falters? Careers do not just come to an end, they change and evolve too. The CEO may become a chairman, an investor, an NED, or maybe a mentor, business coach, or consultant. In this modern world, all have to adapt and all have to open to a process of continuous learning.

The answer to how one evolves and adapts lies with the answer to the question of where their purpose sits and fits. It is very difficult to stop being a leader. Often there is a period of regret and loss after leaving the role, even if successful. Being a leader is a privilege and honor that many feel after leaving the post. It takes time to close that door, to find a new sense of direction and purpose in a career.

One established industry chairman became a crime novelist, opening up a whole new career. Writing had long been his passion, so he followed his dream, once his career was established.

Another leading CEO argued that most CEOs should only have a five-year tenure, as their inspiration and motivation was bound to fall with time. Being a CEO, he argued, was becoming an ever more intense role that one would need to regularly change regardless.

With the speed of advancement and change, all today need to learn and adapt at an even faster rate of change. Everyone will need to be able to adapt and change as a consistent theme. Yes, this may be unsettling but it is also a modern reality. Change is the one constant that we all know is constantly happening. The change experienced in the last 60 years, since 1960, has been immense and it is expected to double in speed with all the advancements in AI. The world will be even more exponentially different by 2040. Most families first had a television in the 1950s only. By the late 1960s, a man had landed on the moon. By the 1970s, most companies had their first computers. By the 1980s, companies were becoming increasingly global. By the mid-1990s, the Internet had started connecting everyone all round the world with easy communications, and global boundaries suddenly opened.

However, despite these changes, many business models have changed very little in the last 20 years and these are now under pressure to change. There are many CEOs who argue that their industries and sectors will not change like others and there are numerous examples of fallen CEOs who have believed such words. All markets, all models are open to change. Change is indiscriminate.

Sharing knowledge has never been more important. Strategic alliances to share ideas and work are essential. No one and no business is an island any more. So why is it that companies are not as open minded to new talents, new voices, and new ideas as they could or arguably should be? Just consider how business has changed in the last decade. Sustainability has become a central theme. The manner in which business works with and within communities and social initiatives have grown in speed and in demand. Expectations are constantly evolving, and the typical customer is also changing at speed.

Might it just be worth charging recruiting teams that possess the ability to think differently? It may well help companies handle the change that is happening all around. It is of course challenging, but the good news is that there is no shortage of great talent ready to serve. The young generation wants to have their opportunity, their chance in the same way that previous generations were given. As business recovers post-Covid-19, all business will need the energy and innovation provided by the young to compliment the guidance of established leaders. This age should see a new alliance between generations emerge as both could learn from the other. The challenge is how to create a framework that would allow this to happen.

CHAPTER 3

Social Renewal

One of the major drivers for change has been the rise of a millennial generation which has yet to truly define itself, although it is clearly making an impact and making a difference. There will be those who argue that they have not broken through as one would have hoped but this is mildly irrelevant.

In most of the advanced economies, the millennials are today the largest group in the working population but this is only part of the equation, for millennials are creating a strong basis for social renewal. They believe in the strength of communities, in local and in a barrier-free conversation when it comes to gender and race. This generation does view the world through very different eyes.

Some argue that the millennials are one of the most diverse, tolerant, educated, and idealistic generations to be seen for some time. However, it is a generation which also carries heavy debt and feels disillusioned with many of the traditional methods. This group can no longer be described as the young, for many are now in their 30s and are positioned to be the leaders of tomorrow who will handle the task of delivering the change that they so desire. In the United States, this generation numbers close to 77 million, so it is no small group to be discounted. It is their idealism though which genuine change can be created and society can once again find a strong balance with new narrative.

The Most Educated of Generations

One of the logical questions to ask is whether the growth in idealism is linked with greater education. It was in the late 1990s, as Tony Blair ran for government, that he spoke of the importance of education being a central piece in his government. "Education, education, education" was his mantra. The argument was simple. The more educated that a society was, the more progressive it would be. It is maybe now that we are beginning to really see the results of that philosophy. It may be with Gen Z that the full potential of the investment in education as a major social tool will be seen, and that is not too far away.

It is not hard to see that each passing generation is more educated than the previous one and also possesses values that they will not compromise upon that little bit more. The Silent Generation set the tone of change with the new narrative of the 1950s and 1960s. So much did change and there was a growth in social consciousness. However, the 1970s was a sober and difficult era which eroded some of the optimism of the 1960s. The Baby Boomers grew up with great ideals but they also had a strong desire to build a better economic and social base which acted as a spur for this generation to become arguably the most successful business generation in history, in terms of wealth generation. They lived the dream released by Ronald Reagan and Margaret Thatcher and their free economics of the 1980s. However, until the 2000s there was an underlying understanding that leaders also held a social responsibility to their employees, teams, and communities. This did change in the 2000s under the influence of a long economic boom period combined with real advancements in technology. The dot com boom suddenly opened the eyes of business that they could compete on the global stage as never before. The importance of an internal culture and community declined as the eyes were toward what could be achieved on a larger scale. The concept of globalization became real and arguably both business and politics started to see a world with less boundaries. However, many wanted those boundaries to remain in place as the danger was that traditions, customs, food styles, and produce would be eroded in the name of global markets.

During the years 2016 to 2020, one could see that there a natural tension arising between the desire for greater globalization and the desire for strong regional identities. In 2014, there was the Scottish Independence Referendum; in 2016, the Brexit vote; and in 2017 to 2018, the Catalan Crisis in Spain. Of course, each had different causes and influences but it is clear that the importance of a region and culture is not something to be either undervalued or undermined.

One would think that with greater education would come even more of a focus on globalization but actually the opposite seems to be true.

There has been a search for one's roots, identity, and history. The more educated the emerging generations seemed to become, the stronger were the social awareness and a greater belief in progressive practices, communities, and localism.

The share of young adults with a bachelor's degree or higher has steadily climbed since 1968. Amongst millennials, around 39 percent of those aged 25 to 37 have a bachelor's degree or higher (18), compared with just 24 percent of Baby Boomers and 15 percent in the previous generation. It is clear that with each passing generation, there is a higher level of the educated emerging.

One of the interesting social changes though is that the share of millennial women with a bachelor's degree is now higher than that of men. It does seem that women particularly have been driven to achieve higher levels.

As noted earlier, this has been a growing trend which saw real progress with the Baby Boom generations. The Baby Boom women really did impact on the workplace in a way that had not happened previously. As early as 1985, more young Boomer women were employed (66 percent) than were not in the labor force (28 percent) (18). This did signal a major change from previous generations.

One of the real complications is that the Baby Boom generation has been perceived to have amassed great wealth. However, the relative earnings of middle management have remained relatively flat over the last 30 years. In hard facts, the millennials have only earned slightly less than in previous generations; the major difference is that previous generations reached positions of leadership at an earlier age and felt far more empowered. Back in the 1980s, it used to be viewed as a fair ambition to aspire to be a director by the age of 30. Today, this would be very unlikely to be achieved. The average age of becoming a director today has increased quite markedly and the average age of becoming a CEO too has risen to 59 (19).

A report (19a) noted that from the year 2005 to 2019, the average age of a CEO rose by 14 years. It is easy to quickly realize that this also meant that the birth date of a CEO in 2005 and 2019 were the same. The Baby Boomers were staying in post longer than previous generations and were clearly less inclined to step aside to free up the next generation's progress.

One can argue the case of earnings between generations, but the real concerns have been the lack of opportunity and the lack of genuine empowerment. Many complain and wonder at the disengagement of the emerging generations without seemingly asking the hard questions of how they would have felt themselves in the same situation. Empowerment used to be one of the most clichés for the development of talent and the evidence would suggest that the Baby Boom generation which was more empowered and enabled prospered as a result. One does wonder how engaged they would have felt if they had been more controlled and less enabled. The prior CEO statistics does suggest that the Baby Boomers have proven themselves to be very able and competent, so one wonders why they want to deprive the emerging generations from the same learning experiences that they had.

Real change is driven through the opportunity to achieve. If this is restrained, then it is very natural that the tensions highlighted in the Vitality report earlier (10) come to the fore. The millennials and Gen Z will acquire wealth as they themselves are empowered and allowed to influence.

A Belief in Localism and Communities

The millennial generation is now beginning to move into positions of influence. Just as with the Baby Boomers, they are now buying homes (even if supported by their parents' wealth), starting companies, creating consumer change, and even changing brand behaviors. They are beginning to enter the political arena, although here too it is notable how dominated this is by those of a previous generation.

As has been noted, the millennials have arguably felt the fallouts from Covid-19 and from the 2008/09 financial crash and this will naturally have impacted on their perspectives. They have embraced the belief in localism which, as an ethos, has grown very much stronger during the Covid-19 lockdown. It is clear that many have a commitment today to a local place almost more than to the overall concept of a nation.

This is a point which was made a couple of years ago in both the United Kingdom and the United States. Many became disillusioned with national politics, so they found hope and a belief in more localized communities and politics. People moved their commitment from the national stage to a more local place, something which could be felt and touched. It was almost as if many felt that national politics lived and operated in a different sphere of life: one which they would not be able to either relate to or influence. It was therefore natural that this led to a move toward greater localism: a belief in local traders, products, and the community.

There will be many that argue that it has been this growing belief which lay beneath the argument for Brexit, for Scottish Nationalism, and for the Spanish unrest in Catalonia. To a level this is true, but it is deeper: it is a desire for daily life to have greater meaning, that communities do once again come together to be the basis of society.

When did this change begin to happen?

Everyone has a different moment that they can point to. In the United Kingdom, many point toward the start of the Blair Government when so many held a firm belief that Blair would create a genuine momentum of change, that politics would change. When it became clear that this would not happen, a disillusionment set in which then came to the fore with the fallout from the Iraq War.

In the United States, many argue that the 2000 Election did leave many feeling disillusioned and of course, the Iraq War confirmed this to many. The Obama presidency promised much but still the hoped-for change did not quite manifest itself.

It is no coincidence that the genuine movements of the last few years have no clear leader: #MeToo, The Extinction Rebellions, even Black Lives Matter. The cause is championed but there appears to be no figure-head as was the case in the days of Martin Luther King or with the great CND marches in London at the start of the 1980s. Does this illustrate the desire to be part of a community rather the need to lead? Does it illustrate the desire for social change but with a difference?

Suddenly what matters is not leadership but real social issues which do impact on daily life. It is one of the contradictions of the emerging generations in that they hold a global view but also a very local one. They want their communities to feel strong, their schools, their hospitals, but less the nation as a whole as they have lost trust in leaders.

Local is beautiful again. It has less to do with nostalgia as some will argue but more to ensuring that life is about more than an individual. It is about belonging to something which has meaning and stands apart from the institutions, which many feel have led to disappointment in politics and companies.

It is remarkably natural. The millennials have been brought up on strong ideals, ideals that they have not seen lived up to by leaders or in business. Of course, they will seek to therefore live these ideals through another route. Communities are about the whole, something which impacts on the daily lives of children, parents, local traders, and craftsmen. It does create a meaning that will naturally build a link to the core ideals that the millennials have been seeking.

In America, the community has long held real meaning. High school sports have long served to bring all the community together in a way that is not the same in other countries. In other countries, communities have all been finding their voice through music, culture, food, wine, history, and long-held traditions. It has seen a renewal in the link between historical traditions and the modern world. Some will say that football has long been the center piece of communities across Europe but this is more tribal and a more male-led approach rather than a center piece for families although this too is gradually changing.

The Age of CPC—Community, Purpose, and Contribution

The other interesting shift is that the millennials want to select their homes where they can see a richness of life, not just what they can access and consume. They want to live amongst communities which create and where they can contribute. It is this desire to contribute to something bigger than themselves which does illustrate the major change in trend.

The challenge for companies is how to ensure that they attract and retain the best talent, but also become organizations which really do tap into this desire for contributing to something more than themselves. This is the heart of the change. No longer is the desire for the best results, the greatest shareholder return, and the greatest wealth the core objective but a balanced perspective takes into account social contribution: to the people employed, to their communities, and to the social structure in which they operate.

Add into this equation, the need for life to possess genuine purpose which allows the individual to love, through action, the ideals with which they expect to live their lives and then, it is the age of *CPC: community, purpose, and contribution.*

So much has been written in recent times about the rise in mental health issues, in anxiety, and in stress. As our research noted, over 40 percent of senior leaders still do struggle to understand that this is a real issue and yet there are so many pieces of research circulating which illustrate the scale of the problem. How can this be the case? How can over40 percent struggle to understand the issue?

For a number of key reasons:

1. As the Vitality report (10) illustrates so well, too high a percentage feel under financial strain. As has been noted, the rewards for senior players have increased at a higher rate than those in lower to middle income levels over the last 10 years. It will naturally create strain and anxiety.

2. The Baby Boomer generation grew up with high ideals but accepted that it would require compromise. They accepted compromise in return for opportunity and wealth. The following generations have grown up with the same ideals but re-enforced through greater education and parental love and the concept of compromise had a different meaning. They grew up expecting their lives to have genuine purpose and meaning.

3. The influence and trust in leadership has been eroded. In the 1980s, there was still a high level of trust in leaders. Leaders, at that time, were also more visible and seemed to believe in something bigger. As this perception has been eroded, the majority have come to believe, rightly or wrongly, that business ethics are poor and self-interest too dominant and have become disengaged. As has been mentioned previously, as business became more invested in by venture capital and institutional investors so it marked a shift away from a traditional community focus to one which was more global with less boundaries and with different aspirations.

It is natural that growth in debt, greater financial strain, and a loss of trust in leadership and business will create increased levels of anxiety and stress. The surprise should not be that 1:4 people will struggle with mental health issues in their lives, but that 40 percent of executives still struggle to understand that companies need to do more today to really ensure that their companies play a bigger role within communities, and that there is genuine purpose which is bigger than profit.

This problem can be easily resolved but it does need leadership teams to begin to think with far greater breadth. This is an era when the largest group in the workforce wants to see progressive actions within their own business, and greater community action externally.

One of the interesting dimensions of change will lie within major cities which have for so long been the major location of jobs. During the Covid-19 lockdown, a number of CEOs have spoken that it could lead to the end of the "skyscraper" office and that more large offices will need to rethink space and perhaps build campuses which create a far stronger employee journey and lifestyle. One example is the CEO of Barclays Bank (20) who commented:

> There will be a long-term adjustment to our location strategy. The notion of putting 7000 people in the building may be a thing of the past.

At the same time, many of the villages within cities have found new senses of communities, energy, and life. In some ways, second- and third-tier areas have also found a new culture which could help revitalize the locality.

Back to Roots Culture

It is of course too soon to draw any conclusions from the Covid-19 crisis but it seems to simply emphasize and highlight a desire that already existed: a desire for many disengaged employees to be able to escape their office environments and find new meaning back in local towns, villages, and communities, whether urban or rural. There are many saying that they have no desire to return to working a full week in the office and will seek greater balance between working from home and in the office. This does lend support to the campus concept as employees want something which is a better experience than travelling to a busy city center office where they already feel disengaged. The challenge for many companies will lie in how they do re-engage talent and build new cultures at the heart of their business.

Of course, many will counter with a belief that this is simply a trend and that hard economics will dictate that people will once again fall in line.

Time will tell but the aforementioned trend is not about Covid-19. Covid-19 has simply been a catalyst to highlight trends that already existed.

It Just Needs New Thinking

This book has made the case that market fallouts in 2008/09 had a negative impact upon productivity and on the engagement of emerging talent. The facts do tend to support this case. It is therefore a reasonable argument to suggest that the same cannot happen again as all that will happen is that productivity will decline further, and it will be ever harder to engage talent. It also disregards the CPC principle outlined previously in the chapter. It is more likely that companies will need to adopt new, broader thing and that HR will need to completely reinvent themselves.

If companies do want to attract and retain the best and brightest talent, then they need to understand both the CPC principle and the "global and local" axis which sits at the center of emerging generations. They do want to create change that does impact on the global environment, to protect it for future generations. However, they also want to see a revival of local communities and cultures. It is all about finding both real meaning and purpose in life, something the emerging generations have been taught to seek by parents and through films and education. They have been taught not to compromise and to keep true to their ideals.

There is a new social energy emerging which is progressive and caring and can help communities all across the world reinvent themselves, create new stories, and find new legacies.

How Does Politics Compete?

One of the interesting questions will be how leaders will need to change and adapt, both in business and in politics.

It has been argued that already many are naturally adapting and ensuring that a social message sits at the heart of their dialog. In Scotland, Nicola Sturgeon has been widely praised for the way in which she has stood up to the Westminster Government and followed her own path. Critics argue that she purposefully opposes every action on principle, but she has built a strong platform in Scotland where many believe she is principled and places community first.

Ironically, it is also argued that Boris Johnson managed to win a handsome victory in the 2019 UK General Election as he managed to by-pass the media bubble and appeal to the average person. He did take Labour's traditional strongholds as he managed to ensure that his message resonated with the average voter. It has been argued that the success of Dominic Cummings, the highly controversial advisor to Prime Minister Johnson, is that he understands the average voter far better than other political advisors who have been sidetracked through other narratives and hence was a key influence in winning both the Leave vote in the 2016 Brexit campaign and in the 2019 General Election. His success was in creating messages and a narrative that impacted effectively on the average person.

Business leadership teams will now need to also adapt and change. The demands on leadership are already changing at speed as is the case for all of the aforementioned trends and the increased vulnerability and uncertainty in daily life. Leaders are moving from being directorial in approach to being listeners, learners, and adapters. They will now need to develop social sustainability agendas within their strategies which ensure that the companies also lead the core principle of community, purpose and contribution.

It could well be that we witness both politics and business coming far closer together again as both will be seeking to impact on the social agenda. It will together see greater support and finance for local and social initiatives. Both will be competing for the engagement and support from millennials and Gen Z who will become far more influential with each passing year.

So, what does this mean? What change are we likely to see?

It is always dangerous to forecast what changes will emerge, but the trends do suggest:

- Stronger alliances between big business and social initiatives. There will be a growth of more not-for-profit businesses emerge.
- A far more progressive agenda to emerge within business which really should break down the remaining barriers and see far more progress for both women and BAME employees
- Gradually and slowly, traditional social barriers will break down.
- HR needs to and should reinvent themselves to once again focus on the development of human capital and also address how employees can find purpose in their careers.
- Leadership will naturally evolve and change as millennials move into positions of authority. However, the skills of a leader will evolve and be far less directorial and far more focused on establishing the mission and purpose of a company as it will be this that engages investors and talent
- In time, business leaders and politicians will regain trust through far better communications and actions
- There will be a revival of localism; with new traditions and crafts emerging, communities will be stronger.
- Creativity will become increasingly popular. It sits at the heart of finding purpose in life so logically this should be a natural consequence.

Given all the facts, the aforementioned are logical conclusions to draw. One of the core arguments has been that the emerging generations are being defined but they are in fact redefining the institutions that they are disengaged by and wish to leave. That has been the story of recent times and of course, it is logical that these institutions will simply adapt and re-engage in time. This will naturally mean change and how that change appears can be debated.

The traditional institutions are needed. They are the core pillars on which the economy and society are founded. Strong business is needed, and effective political leadership is needed too. They have survived and endured many long crises before. They simply need to learn and believe in a new narrative, one which places society, localism, and people right back at the heart. It could well be that doing this politics finds a new lease of life as localism does rely on democracy, so the principle could be finding new strength.

There is a strength in localism as it does naturally create a stronger social infrastructure, family units, health, and well-being and supports the development of local small businesses which are often the bedrock to strong economies.

AI and the Community

The interesting battle will be between the undoubted advancements in AI and how this impacts on the aforementioned. The prevailing argument of the moment is that companies will find the balance between AI and people and that this balance will support employees in finding extra time to interact socially, both in the company and within communities.

There is little doubt that, in theory, AI/technology should allow for greater individual freedom, higher levels of communication, and greater opportunity to interact with both friendship groups and colleagues. However, the question is whether the tools are being used effectively.

Many blame social media for a whole range of social woes and problems but research actually suggests that it is the lack of face-to face contact which is where the problem lies. The same is true in relation to the work environment. All the evidence suggests that many are working longer hours, with higher levels of anxiety. There is clearly a learning needed to ensure that a far better balance is found Arguably the lockdown period created such a learning to take place as suddenly many found they could work from their homes, in spaces they found safe, that anxiety levels fell and work sickness levels too.

As with many advancements, it takes time to learn how the best balance can be found. Many have taken the advancements that technology offered without understanding that it could also mean changing traditional structures, processes, and approaches.

Many are already arguing that the greatest positive to come from the Covid-19 lockdown has been that it has been proven that work can continue very effectively from home using technological advancement. Many companies needed to adapt and change within days and they were able to do to good technological processes. Others also argue that we are not many years away from seeing the advent of a four-day working week which again will support all the aforementioned.

All the previously listed information appear to be fair and sound arguments. The counter argument is that, as much as AI is rapidly adopted, many are becoming weary of the ever faster, more transparent nature of the world. They want a sense of wholeness in their lives, wholeness built from healthy relationships, responsibility, belonging, and an identifiable role. They want the personal again involved in communities and this naturally asks for real conversations in real-time, real meals around real tables, and real problem-solving and sacrifice, less hash-tagging.

There is a lot of evidence of this within hospitality, prelockdown, as more and more wanted to come together over dinner and experience different foods, and the concept of "breaking bread" was growing across communities.

The Opportunity for Hospitality

All the aforementioned can mark an exciting opportunity for hospitality in so many ways and on so many levels.

- As has already been outlined, hotels and restaurants can become the ambassadors for engaging external audiences about the culture and heritage of the community. Audiences today seek ever greater authentic storytelling and experiences; hotels and restaurants can do this very effectively and even through using local foods and products.
- Hotels can play a leading role in communities as an employer, in supporting initiatives, using local produce and suppliers, in playing a genuine leadership role. Hotels, restaurants, and pubs can be a strong pillar to help bring communities together.

- Food, of course, has become a universal language and does serve to educate about cultures and bring people together. Food can be a common glue that serves to support communities
- There is a major trust and belief in localism and so it is good business for hotels and restaurants to work with and support local producers
- Hospitality can be a role model industry in terms of employment, in the creation of opportunity for people from all backgrounds and groups.
- In food service within businesses, it can be food that really does help to bring people together and help create the culture of a business. Food service will play an increasingly important role in how it supports companies in how they re-engage talent and teams to come back to offices.
- If the campus concept does progress, it will support the services which will be central in creating employee journeys that engage and inspire people to stay on campus.
- People want personal contact once again. People want to see greater respect and care, and nothing says nor shows this more than service.
- In schools, there will be increased focus on combating obesity, health, and diet. Food service will become ever more important.
- As will be outlined in a later chapter, diets will change and will be ever more demanding and varied and ultimately play increasingly more important roles in life.

The opportunity for hospitality is huge. It has it all within its own hands to showcase just how influential an industry and business it can be. The challenge, as always, is taking it. If it can take the opportunity, then the industry can be viewed as progressive and advance its cause and perception. It can be more attractive to investors and to talent, failing which it would have missed a golden opportunity to be an industry that it has long aspired to be.

CHAPTER 4

Cultural Sustainability

Cultural sustainability is so often overlooked and yet just may be one of the most important of the four core pillars. As more people look toward seeking something which is genuine and authentic, so they are turning their eyes toward their heritages and roots. Culture sits right at the center of this search and is something that everyone does relate to in one form or another. It may be music. It may be history. It may be literature or theater. For some it lies in their farms, vineyards, their food, wine, and produce. In recent years, there are many communities who have been seeking to renew their links to the past and many who want to find their own roots, their own heritage which too is represented by culture.

Cultural sustainability is all about maintaining cultural beliefs, cultural practices, heritage conservation, and culture as its own entity. One of the arguments presented through this book is that hotels, resorts, restaurants, and bars can play a far more proactive role in telling the story of their communities' history and cultural legacy. As guests seek ever greater experiences, it is a natural link for hospitality to be a representative of the culture of their region.

The former Michelin star chef, Christian Delteil, offered some fascinating insight into how gastronomy sits at the heart of France's regional cultures in a deeper level than in most other countries and therefore, the French do not feel threatened at all by the advancements in gastronomy made in other countries:

Food in France has always been a central part of the culture. In France one eats and when you have finished, your next thought is of what will be your next meal. Food is more important to the French than to nearly any other nation. Everyone thinks they are a Michelin inspector. This is a major problem when you try to run your own business and try to please people. People don't tip, it's all included in the price, and that could be the cause of some problems in the customer service.

I left France in 1975 and returned in 2011 and spent 36 years of my professional life in the UK. I had forgotten was that in France the real roots of French Gastronomy lie in regional and local cooking. It has never been a trend or fashion, it's real, genuine, authentic and each county is proud of their regional cooking and wine. It lies within the soul of each provence.

One of the relatively new trends is the re-birth of the Fait Maison. The French government has even issued a new logo for restaurants: "Fait Maison" or "Home Made" promotes and controls/ensures that a restaurant who says it cooks everything on site does use fresh produce to do so. There is no compromise.

Traditionally brasserie food is society's central focus; good food and great value. French gastronomy will always be the benchmark for others to measure themselves as in France it is not about clever ideas and innovation but about real food that has exceptional taste. All we need to improve in France is the concept of service with a smile. There seems to be a lot of focus on service across different sectors in France. At last, we are seeing a step towards progressing in an area where we do need to improve.

On saying all the above, I am not blind to the changes taking place. Like many countries, French eating habits have been shaken. With more people travelling the world and discovering new cultures, eating habits are changing and people are more demanding. French restaurateurs in major cities have to embrace and follow this trend. The situation is not the same in the country side where the majority of customers are still very attached to their regional and local food, and where tourists still want to eat French local specialities and local wine—they want France!

The restaurants industry's new word is "Bistronomie"—bistro food with an emphasis on high quality products, texture and flavours. The burger seems to be making a big come back. Burger King has announced great development plans in France. Sushi restaurants, organic and vegetarian restaurants are popular as well. The food truck concept is just beginning to make its debut

but, in my opinion, it will very soon come to saturation in major cities. Another interesting and growing concept is Class Croute. Started 25 years ago Class Croute addresses the restaurant market in major business parks and offices. The restaurants provide breakfast, lunch, and afternoon snack from Monday to Friday and are closed in the evening. One of their mottos is "Good food is not a luxury".

Through food, customers will look for different experiences, new flavours and new textures. While eating, customers want to travel and want to experience going back in time to see old traditions. In the current market, restaurants offering exotic, authentic and quality cuisine with good value for money will be the winners.

It was Mark Twain, when he read of his death, remarked "The reports of my death are greatly exaggerated". It is the same with French gastronomy. It will never die as it means so much in everyday life. It will have its challenges but it will stay true to its roots, its beliefs, the tastes that has made French food stand apart for many decades and evolve. French cooking does not need to change.

Christian Delteil's comments are important as they reflect just how important, how much pride, can be created by a close bond between hospitality and regional legacies.

Across all countries, hospitality can play such an important role. It is already fulfilling the role through food, wine, beer and spirits. It is simply taking this to another level and telling the cultural story through art, music, dance, and storytelling. It has been well documented that storytelling has become so much more powerful as so many are seeking to find a meaning or link to something that they can relate to. Storytelling has become a central feature of daily life as audiences want to be engaged by great stories that inspire, create awe, and leave lasting memories. It does explain the recent successful re-emergence of the Marvel characters in film as they tell stories that do engage. This is extreme but at the other end of the scale, many want to re-engage in the great stories of the past, of myths, and of historical events. In so many ways, it could be an exciting opportunity for those who grasp the opportunity. Hotels and resorts can tell the stories of their localities through art on the walls, through curated experiences, through wine tasting, through craft studios.

Of course, the word culture means different things to different people. For some, it is represented by art and museums, historical landscapes. For others it is deeper: a set of beliefs, morals, methods, and knowledge passed down from one generation to another. The most obvious examples are food recipes, techniques in making crafts, and the growing of crops and wines. It is the knowledge that lies within a region which in previous generations many felt was being eroded by the constant drive toward globalization. The more global each country became, so local knowledge would be lost. As the early 2000s have been dominated by such a move toward globalization, it is fascinating to see a move back toward respect and care for the knowledge which exists within families and communities.

In many ways, the concept of cultural sustainability is also the underlying story of this book. Founded as a concept in the mid-1990s, it has been the least powerful voice of the four central pillars in sustainability. The advancement of the Internet and political structures has seen a consistent move toward globalization. The voice for cultural sustainability was almost forgotten but through tourism and resorts. However, the drive toward globalization, as powerful as it has been, has also left so many feeling that they have lost something deeper and of value. We have written of the move toward localism; culture is all part of this same movement. Sustaining and maintaining cultural practices gives many a greater sense of themselves, their history, and roots. It could very well sit at the heart of the actions of many when arguing for Brexit, for Scottish Independence, against the EU, for the independence of Catalonia, and more. One can see the same trends emerge all across the world combined with a stronger and greater respect for traditions.

As forgotten as cultural sustainability may seem, it does impact very strongly on both social and political sustainability. Politicians will appeal to their history and roots to connect with their electorates. Social communities are founded and glued together often by their traditions.

The greatest problem that cultural sustainability faces is that history and tradition are both very real but can also be quite vague. While the connection is often emotional, it is also the actual knowledge which is passed down from one generation to another. This includes food, music, and dance. These very factors create an influence and connection within a society. It is reflective of society.

Often when one thinks about cultural sustainability, one will think of museums, art galleries, libraries, opera houses, heritage sites, and theaters. All these are important, but these are just one part of the equation; it is also the day-to-day things that live within a community. Cultural sustainability is why many argue today that food is the one true universal language and can break down barriers, and why others celebrate great regional wines; or find great joy in local music and dance traditions. Culture speaks to the soul and to our desire for finding experiences that are deeper, authentic, and memorable.

The Eurovision Song Contest (21)

The Eurovision Song Contest has become increasingly popular around the world; it is quirky, eccentric, and unusual. This may seem a strange thing to write about at this juncture and understandably so. In the early years of the contest, the United Kingdom used to be a very competitive force and would be regularly near the top of the voting. It attracted many of the country's leading singers including Sandie Shaw, Cliff Richard, and Lulu. However, as it grew in success, it attracted more countries to enter, became increasingly diverse and eccentric, and the United Kingdom became less competitive. Many blamed politics as the United Kingdom was often not a good political ally to many countries across Europe. However, this was too simplistic. It is easy to blame the United Kingdom's fall in popularity on politics and being a proud island nation, often in conflict with the EU.

However, British music has been hugely popular all across the world for long periods of time. This success has not been diminished by politics, so where does the issue lie?

The Eurovision Song Contest has become reflective of many of the highly varied cultural traditions of Europe's countries. As such, it is very natural that countries which are connected by land, and often share a more connected history, will have more connection in music than with the United Kingdom. People will naturally vote for a culture and tradition which they relate to, and as Europe is mainly connected by land

and culture, more than the United Kingdom, the decline is absolutely natural. It will have its moments of success again in the United Kingdom when its songs resonate across cultures, but success is probably determined by those songs which do have cultural links and possess broad cultural appeal.

The Link Between Cultural Sustainability and Tourism

The obvious major relationship in cultural sustainability is with tourism. This is central to the economies of many parts of the world, most especially island economies. Culture and heritage define people from all around the world and these act as an attraction in tourism. There is a natural and growing relationship between culture, heritage, sustainability, and environment. A tourism strategy should mix the legacies of the past with the needs and desires of the future.

To place into context, in Greece tourism relates to 20.4 percent of GDP (22), attracting 33 million tourists in 2018. The global average impact is just over 10 percent. In Italy, tourism equates to just over 13 percent (23). In France, in contrast, it equates to just 9.7 percent (24). In the United States, it equates to 2.6 percent (25). To place in fair context as these figures are against GDP, France is the most visited country in the world with 86 million, the United States third most with 76 million, and Italy fifth with 58 million. All these countries have unique experiences which engage visitors and have cultural heritages which are strong.

From these figures alone, it is easy to see a clear correlation between resorts, culture, history, and tourism.

What does this mean in practice for hospitality?

A number of points:

- Resorts will become ever more advanced and often secluded. As the world becomes increasingly vulnerable, so many visitors will simply not wish to stray away from secure locations. Resorts therefore become the central focus for the guest experience which will need to include the most advanced skills in comfort and luxury, but also with access to the cultural heritage of the past.

- ○ One good example of such a resort could prove to be The Birch Hotel Resort, Hertfordshire, England, which is aiming to be a retreat that allows guests to escape urban life. It lies only 30 minutes away from London and aims to retain the guest onsite for the duration of their stay with family cinema areas, wellness spas, a pottery studio, an art studio, a farm, a vegetable garden, and 55 acres of prepared landscape.

- ○ Another example could be the great resorts of Borgo Egnazia in Puglia and the Verdura Resort in Sicily which both offer the attractions to remain onsite but also genuinely curated experiences to allow guests to discover the true experience of the regions but in the safest of ways. Puglia is famous for its olive groves and also the famous old ancient huts (the Trulli) which date back to the Middle Ages, local breads and pastas, its local wines, and long coastline. The guest to Puglia cannot be influenced by its links to history and local cultures.

- In cities, all across the world, hotels could well become the voice of the community so that guests can learn and experience the traditions of the local history whilst in a secure and comfortable setting. Just as with Puglia, hotels can tell the stories of local traditions, customs, and foods.

- Tourism plays an increasingly important role in that it can educate and inform, break down poor perceptions, and create greater understanding among cultures. The overall experience which is generated and created will therefore be ever more impactful in the larger objective of creating greater understanding between cultures.

- Those that work in tourism have a responsibility to protect the local culture and traditions whilst, at the same time, maximizing revenue flows. It is a naturally fine line to walk. Protection of the environment and culture is going to need new strategies.

- Will new service lines evolve through the development of the previously mentioned information? The underlying theme is all about creating greater connections between people drawn from different societies. Service is the key to personal care. How will service change and evolve alongside developments in cultural sustainability?

- There is an ever greater need to protect historic sites. This, of course, adds extra cost as heritage sites need to be protected and also to create a unique experience when visited. It is interesting that just as localism has become more important so has history. There is a growing desire for people to feel a link to the past, to history, to great stories that made the present be as it is. The great heritage sites become the key global face of many cities: the Coliseum in Rome, the Eiffel Tower in Paris, the Taj Mahal in India, Buckingham Palace in London. How does one create an ever greater customer experience for the guest?

  o Italy is arguably one of the most loved countries in the world, not just by its own people but by visitors. The core reason is that it has successfully been able to marry simple yet exceptional food styles, great wines, beautiful countryside, and history. Take, for example, the romance of Capri, Venice, and its canals, the marriage of history and art in Florence, and the great history and architecture of Pisa, Genoa, and Rome. France too follows closely behind with its own blend of fabulous regional food styles, the greatest wines, and variety in environment from Provence to Loire to Bordeaux to Brittany to the great cities of Paris and Lyon.

  o The United Kingdom has often lagged behind. It has been a common discussion point that the United Kingdom has often not been as strong as other countries in presenting itself on the world stage and yet it does possess some superb world-class attractions which include the great sporting events at Wimbledon, Ascot, Henley, Lords, Wembley, and Twickenham. The United Kingdom has the greatest global sporting stage to mix with its tradition. It brings in an estimated annual revenue of £23.8 billion to the U.K. economy. On top, the United Kingdom has a full range of beautiful landscapes which are still relatively unknown to the international traveller: the Highlands, the Cotswolds, the Norfolk broads, the Yorkshire Dales, the Lake District. All have great stories to tell, great local histories, food styles, produce, and beers. It can rival France for its regional differences and interest, but France is far stronger in how it engages and markets itself.

o The desire for a connection with history was perhaps best illustrated by how the Scottish economy gained from Mel Gibson's film "Braveheart" in the mid-1990s. It has also served as a greater call for nationalism.

It is a change of mindset. Every country has a great story to tell that needs to be told through guest experiences and through strong cultural sustainable programs. It is an interesting thought that cultural sustainability is the almost forgotten partner of the four leading pillars in sustainability and yet could be the most long term, impactful, and important.

Leading Change Through Food

There is a strong argument that hospitality is a leading force in supporting social change, through cultural legacy, in how we embrace the variety of cuisines from around the world in restaurants and food service. While this is true, there is still greater opportunity.

It is food today that arguably educates societies about other cultures and breaks down barriers in a way that very few other factors are able to achieve. Food brings people together. There is an increased desire to experiment and learn about other cultures through food. It creates a basis for greater social understanding, acceptance, and learning. It may be simply a catalyst, but it plays a very important role today in bridging social differences and allowing for more progressive thought.

Food has long been a central social glue. One can look back to the days of the Greek Empire and history tells us that food and dining as a group was as much about enjoying company and conviviality as it was about the cuisine. This continued throughout the Roman Era, during which the convivium (Roman dinner party) became a mainstay in society.

There have been numerous studies which have shown that people who eat together share higher levels of trust and togetherness than those who do not. This is one of the great challenges and opportunities for food service companies which operate within companies and in schools; Loneliness and mental health issues can be combated through great food service which serves to bring people together. This does mark a new, evolving narrative as there is a growing understanding that the decline in face-to-face contact is one of the root causes of the increase in loneliness and anxiety. Moreover as people become fitter and more healthy, diets are naturally changing and companies have a role to play in supporting good health.

If one goes to war-torn areas, one will often find great foods styles and see how it brings a simple joy to faces. Go to the most intense work environments, and it is food that brings a smile to the face and creates informal communications that often solves problem. Walk round the great village areas in New York, Paris, Rome, or London in an early evening and see the genuine joy and energy that exudes from the restaurants.

It is a simple truth; food is the one universal language and today plays an ever more important role. It sits at the heart of social interaction, just as it sits at the center of most health and well-being strategies.

If one looks at the United Kingdom, it had, in 2019, the fiercest battle over Brexit and yet still there is a real love for the food of migrants that have played such an important role in the United Kingdom's recent history. Indian food is often classed as the most popular "British" cuisine. Italian is in the top four.

Across all societies, food stands apart. Japanese cuisine is even considered a World Heritage as it plays a role in society that goes beyond the actual meal. Seasonal food is important for society, because the diet is based on each season of the year. To stay healthy throughout the year, Japanese children learn important values and skills such as cooperation, teamwork, and responsibility in their school lunches during elementary school. Bento boxes (lunch boxes) influenced, to some extent, the personality of Japanese children either by helping them to socialize easier with their classmates or by excluding them out of a group. A meal in Japan is very important to society, because there is more to just eating the food; there are several rules and etiquettes to follow. A meal in Japanese society goes beyond food, because through a meal people can socialize, build stronger bonds, cooperate, work in teams, and help society to develop. It is also a way to thank gods in rituals. Traditional food in modern society is very important to keep the culture.

Food has not always enjoyed the "love" that it does today but one has to understand the changes that have taken place across our leisure time. Films today seem less about a story and more about dramatic visuals. Social media is often about personalities. Sport is today often less about simple fun and playing in the garden or street and is now almost an important part of our daily disciplines. We know there is a growing lack of trust in the traditional social pillars. Food is the one thing that is still about simple joy and how we bring our friends together.

One of the most constant discussions within businesses is over the cost of their food service. It is well known that food service was almost commoditized but it plays today an important role in impacting the daily lives from the top to the bottom. It impacts everything from productivity to wellness to friendships/loneliness to informal communications to fighting obesity. It is no longer just about food but how it does impact and go beyond the meal itself.

It is the heart of social interaction which every business needs and wants. It can be the core of culture and business.

This is arguably even more important within the education system. There is increasing acceptance that the need to nurture the young is not simply confined to education; in fact, it includes everything that surrounds the entire system. Schools have been working hard to create new solutions which aim to support young people in daily life. This includes helping to create new processes that develop mental robustness, strong life skills, and a greater understanding of good diet and nutrition. There is a genuine enthusiasm and demand for change, as well as for the need to ensure young people are being nurtured as effectively as possible.

The food service sector sits right at the center of this drive, and companies are becoming increasingly aware that their remit can be far wider reaching than has traditionally been the case. Food service today really does impact directly on diet and nutrition, and it is an important ally in combating both obesity and mental health issues. Indeed, schools and educational establishments all over are reintroducing cookery lessons back into the school curriculum in order to teach important life skills alongside the benefits of effective teamwork.

Could this herald the start of a new golden era for food service, one in which it plays an ever higher profile role in daily life? Food is one of the few genuine universal languages today; it brings people together and fosters a genuine sense of joy in daily life.

In a world which has over 7,000 languages, it is very natural that it can be food that can help support the challenges which we face in diversity, in workplaces, and in society at large. There are many studies which show that those who eat together are often healthier, benefit from lower levels of depression and obesity, and have higher levels of self-esteem.

In the great International cities, many take immense pride in the broad variety of food styles and how it can bind cultures together into one bustling cosmopolitan area. London and New York are both major cultural centers of the world through food. Most of the restaurants attract custom from all cultures and both cities are a celebration of globalization. It is through food that we are seeing cultural fusions come together. It is not just London and New York but also other modern international cities such as Dubai and Singapore. It is easy to understand why, as these centers are full of immigrant populations.

Research shows that there is a direct correlation between high-skilled immigration and an increase in the level of innovation and economic performance in cities and regions. Singapore makes a great case study. This South-East Asian island, with a population of just over 5 million, is today one of the globe's heavyweight financial centers. It scores highly in international rankings for areas as diverse as education and ease of doing business, and has been recognized as the world's most technology-ready nation. Singapore is also highly multicultural, with an ethnic mix of people from Chinese, Malay, and Indian descent as well as large populations of different religious faith groups including Buddhists, Christians, Muslims, and Hindus.

When Singapore achieved independence in 1965, its founding fathers instituted measures that would not leave racial harmony to chance. Singapore aggressively promoted racial and ethnic integration. One important measure was its housing policy, which ensured that every public housing complex followed a national quota of racial percentage. This forced people of different ethnicities to learn to live with each other and broke up all the ethnic ghettos that were prevalent at the time of independence. These seemingly autocratic measures have served the small island nation well in producing a well-integrated populace that values meritocracy more than race or religion. Singapore's ethnic and religious diversity has proven to be an asset to the country, and the result is relative racial harmony.

Cultural Diversity

Of course, the most difficult and complex issue is the topic of diversity. It is easy to write that the emerging generations do not see gender and race in the same way as previous generations but of course it is far more complex. In the United Kingdom, the favorite cuisine is actually Indian (27). In a survey of over 2,000 respondents, just over 21 percent cited curry as their favorite dish. It does illustrate just how Indian cuisine has become central within United Kingdom's daily life, even if many curry recipes have been naturally adapted for the pallet of a new audience. There will be similar examples all across the world which reinforce the idea that cultures do come together around food.

Things are changing, as can be seen by the fact that so many view curry as their favorite dish. Step by step, barriers are being broken down and greater understanding is coming together. However, there is still a long road to travel.

There is understandably a natural tension and contradiction at the heart of the debate. Many more want to have renewed value in localism, in tradition, in legacies which naturally serve to push away cultural cohesion between new groups. The challenge lies in how the cultures of minority groups are accepted within the culture as a whole as can be seen by the prior Indian example.

How do we ensure that cultural sustainability is both respectful of the past and considerate of future integration? It is the challenge of being both local and global. The glue which does allow this to be achieved will be cultural.

Societies today are driven often by minority groups. They possess the desire and hunger to be accepted, to make a difference. It is one of the ironies that minorities feel excluded and yet their impact is often central.

It is the minority groups which often create stronger and more diverse attraction economies.

There is substantial research to show that diversity brings many advantages to any society: often increased profitability and creativity, stronger work ethics, and better problem-solving abilities. Peoples with diverse backgrounds bring to bear their own perspectives, ideas, and experiences, helping to create a society which is varied, resilient, and effective, and which outperform those societies which do not invest in supporting diversity.

One of the genuine opportunities that the hospitality industry possesses is how to be the central point of communities and be able to play a major social role. Hospitality does have a role to play in bringing these communities together again post Coronavirus:

We pride ourselves on how we bring people together and then we talk in big terms about the importance of our brand. It is all about people and it should be. Business has evolved in many ways—often in good ways—but we should not forget the founding pillar of hospitality, to bring people together and to care for them. If we forget about our communities we serve, then it will be our loss.

I believe that hotels take a lot from our communities so we should become a part of the community. It could be for charity, sitting on local committees, inviting people to local meetings, giving them a glass of wine, becoming their friend. It is a very exciting part of being a leader, to lead your people in supporting communities.

—Michael Gray, former Regional VP for Hyatt in London

It is a view which is supported by others:

There is no question over this. We have to influence and support communities and schools. The service has to be adapted so that it is part of the community. It is a real opportunity and will need some new thinking.

—Marc Dardenne CEO, Luxury Brands, Europe at Accor

It is not just hotels, I believe we all have a responsibility to give back to our communities and to be conscious of the impact we are making on society. Hotels are such a critical part of any community—they are a microcosm of the local culture; they are often a large employer within the local community and they are a major economic driver for that community. As such, hotels have a responsibility to give back and improve communities in which they call home.

—Martin Rinck, EVP and Chief Brand Officer
at Hilton in Vancouver

I have no doubt that hotels play a key social role in the world and more in local environments. It is essential to increase our focus on how we aid our local community as well as our impact on the environment.

—Ronen Nissenbaum, President and CEO, Dan Hotels

The prior information does highlight again the theme of thinking local as well as global. Hospitality is a business which can be both, a global brand which can act locally, with care, in service.

There has been a conflict between the evolution in business models and maintaining a focus on people. Investors in the future will take the lead from the changes taking place in public priorities and the renewal of major values. There will be more pressure placed on organizations to really invest in sustainability and in contributing to social good.

At the same time, there is a growing recognition that just as leaders need to think about their external responsibilities, so do they need to provide more active support to the development of emerging leaders. A chasm between the generations has emerged, one which does need to be bridged.

CHAPTER 5

Change to the Work Place

How work patterns and workplaces change over the next few years could be one of the most influential areas to impact sustainability. How business views its role in the broader remit of sustainable development will also be absolutely central and fundamental to any real change. We have written about sustainable business and of course this will impact on the workplace, but how?

One of the challenges of the last decade has been the so-called absence of real values and culture within companies. C-Suite executives have talked of culture, but the truth is that very few companies have invested in ensuring that their companies possess strong values. Back in the 1990s, every business understood the importance of how its own culture would drive performance and productivity. The term "cultural fit" was central to most recruitment strategies. Over the past decade however, this has been gradually eroded through M&A, through technology, process, and job boards. We have all read the statistics on how many people have become disengaged. So how is all this reversed and changed?

Business has been primarily about results and the return provided to their shareholders. However, the narrative has been under pressure to change for a number of key reasons:

- During the 2008/09 crash, this singular approach was understandable, but it lost support and trust as it did not deviate even as economies recovered and performed strongly. Everything is about a fine balance and this balance was arguably lost through the quest for greater profits and wealth. Even this could have been effective if the gulf between leadership teams and middle/lower levels had not grown wider. One of the great successes of the John Lewis Partnership is that it is founded on a core principle that the employees should share in the success of the company and that they can trust in this principle. John Lewis's ownership structure was established by a pioneering businessman called John Spedan Lewis, whose father founded the business in 1864. He signed away his ownership rights in 1929 to allow future generations of employees to take forward his "experiment in industrial democracy." His ideas are set out in the company's constitution, which at its heart has the idea of establishing a "better form of business" (28). It has long been viewed as one of the United Kingdom's most respected concerns.

- The emerging generations do want to believe in ideals which are bigger than themselves. This includes the central pillars of environment, community, diversity, and inclusion. They will make buying decisions based on a belief in brands that uphold and support such principles.
- The facts have shown very clearly that this generation has lost faith in its elder generations and wants a quiet drive for change.
- The desire now is for genuine and authentic messages, no spin, but real idealism at the heart.
- Millennials may have a different view of how they would like to work, but they still retain respect for the more experienced generations in the workforce. They want to work for people who will inspire them to do great work. They're not inspired by things like money or status, but rather by core competencies and personality traits.

Whether experienced leaders like it or not, the future lies in their hands. They do want to see change toward a kinder world. Abigail Tan, Chief Executive of the St. Giles Group of Hotels, which runs hotels in New York, London, and Malaysia and who is viewed to be an emerging leader, noted in an interview for this book that:

Some of the reasons for change (in leadership) I believe is the entrance in the general workforce and leadership roles of Xennials and Millennials. Natives of a more interconnected world, both generations respond to a collaborative, shared leadership style, where input from all team members, regardless of "role" is not just welcomed, but actively encouraged. Another reason for change is the pace of society—our world moves at a digital speed and knowledge is ever evolving; therefore, decision making has been decentralised to adapt to the need for quick and informed actions.

The role of leadership has evolved from having a dominant figure who enforces rule and power, top down, to a leader who delegates and empowers to create other leaders within the organisation. Structures have gone from a sharp hierarchy triangle, to one that looks wider and flatter.

Leaders today need to create the vision and set the direction, while motivating and engaging the team to deliver that vision. This has become a more inclusive and collaborative process rather than exclusive.

Although the emergence of this generation is of genuine importance, it is nothing new—more a reconnection with values lost over the last 40 years. There was a strong idealism that lay at the heart of rebuilding economies after World War II. In the 1960s, a whole new narrative emerged talking of ideals which had never been spoken of previously via music and The Beatles, The Rolling Stones, and the Rock Revolution.

The major difference with the millennials is that it is arguably the first generation ever which does believe in equality between genders and race. This is a major shift in mindsets. The attitude of the millennial generation, which will have the most impact on daily lives, is the distinctive and historically unprecedented belief that there are no inherently male or female roles in society. This belief stems directly from millennials' experience of growing up in families in which the mother and father took on roughly equal responsibilities for raising their children.

The Baby Boom generation was the first whereby often both parents held roles and had their own incomes. The Baby Boomers do take a lot of criticism but in truth, they are the generation which did free up the role of women. Baby Boomers were just as idealistic as those in the emerging generations. The difference is that the Baby Boomers grew up in an era which saw tough recessions, the early 1990s, the 2008 crash, and now

Covid-19 impact, and were the first to be able to attain genuine wealth. After growing up in a tougher decade in the 1970s, they were prepared to work hard and to compete to build wealth.

The millennials grew up believing in the ideals given to them by their parents who at heart did believe in a better world. As is natural, the millennials are just a reflection of the Baby Boomers. Today's emerging generation enters the workforce on an equal footing with a natural belief in gender neutrality which will force major changes in the work place, a change that many have wanted.

The biggest difference is that today's millennial women refuse to accept any restrictions, based on their gender or color, on what they might be allowed to do, and on what they may be able to achieve. They believe that they should be free to achieve whatever their ability allows. This is perhaps the first generation to be able to have such a strong belief.

The millennial generation is the first in which women are more likely to attend and graduate from college and professional schools than are men. These achievements have produced a generation of educated, self-confident women who, unlike many of their Boomer mothers and grandmothers, do not see themselves in conflict or competition with men.

The biggest change is that this will be the first generation whereby both partners are genuine equals in how they view the world and in what they expect in return. This could be a generation that does truly free up far more talent and more leaders which in turn will create its own change and opportunities.

At the heart lies the same idealism that their parents possessed when they started out their journeys. The Baby Boomers compromised but the millennials may be a new generation to live out their ideals through action. They do believe in something bigger than themselves

Millennials and Inclusion

As has been previously noted, this generation is already creating genuine social impact with a new perspective and new thinking. In previous times, the whole diversity issue was defined through a number of metrics which included race figures, demographics, equality, and representation.

Millennials view diversity as an integration of varying experiences, different backgrounds, and individual perspectives. It is the same when it comes to the issue of inclusion.

This does impact particularly on employers and companies as their expectation is that the workplace will be a supportive environment which gives a voice to different perspectives on a given issue, from the leadership to front-line employees. Of course, the harsh truth is that the workplace is still some way away from this level.

The perspective and expectations of the millennial generation is exciting in that it will lead to inevitable change. However, it does also highlight how far there is to travel. It does once again stress the need for HR to really step forward and help support the need for change.

Diversity—The Real Game Changer

Of course, leadership in society is not just about the role that the industry plays with external audiences, but also how it is a leading light for its own people. It does have a genuine social role to play once again. Included in the modern challenge of leadership is to ensure that the landscape will encourage talent from all parts of society to emerge. Leadership has a role to ensure that all talent has the opportunity to be seen and to grow.

One of the reasons for the increased tensions that exist between leadership teams and emerging leaders is that there is a whole new philosophy and mindset which has arisen, one which does believe in the value of diverse teams and of inclusion, where all talent is equal and valued. This may sound obvious but is a major step forward which has taken place over the last 10 years and naturally enough, it does serve to create tensions.

It is very important for the industry to become increasingly diverse. I would like to see greater change in age, as well as gender and in ethnic backgrounds. In hospitality, we don't have a problem up to a certain level. I never felt constrained by the fact I was a woman. I do believe that you need the best person for the job and that is all that matters. What I don't agree with is positive discrimination. It is more about removing all barriers in allowing great talent to be able to reach senior levels and let talent and culture flow. This would then offer wonderful opportunities.

—Vicky La Trobe, Consultant

In the United States, 20 percent of board roles are now with women (29). This may not seem very good but it is up from 17 percent in 2018 and 10 percent at the start of the decade. In the United Kingdom, women now hold a third of board positions in the country's top public companies. There is still a way to go but is a step forward. More importantly, it is a level of equality that millennials desire and expect.

In the United Kingdom, just 8 percent of boards have BAME board directors (30) which has seen no improvement over the last two years; 47 percent of companies have no BAME at board level (31). However, the number of Fortune 500 companies with greater than 40 percent diversity has more than doubled from 69 to 145 since 2012 (32).

If the "MeToo" campaign and momentum has proven anything, it is that there is a desire for change and what was once acceptable no longer is. The emerging generations do expect to see greater understanding, diversity, and inclusion across all businesses. This does mark a whole new era.

People are the foundation for success. It is important to build a diverse team across all levels to ensure optimal value of mindshare, creativity and most importantly, perspective. When you cultivate an environment that encourages diverse perspective you also gain a culture of learning, collaboration and innovation. This partnered with a team committed to a common goal is a truly remarkable experience to be part of. (Martin Rinck, Chief Brand Officer, Hilton)

Future books, written on industry leadership, may well look back at this era as the time when the balance was readdressed, when companies did start to reinvest back into people once again to ensure that their companies attracted the best talent and retained them through being diverse and inclusive. There is genuinely no excuses left for progress not to become stronger and more at the forefront of company strategies.

Some will counter and argue that a fall in GDP and economies, following Coronavirus, will stall change but the hard facts are showing time and again that diversity and inclusion do equal stronger performance and bottom-line results. It may well heighten the drive toward change.

The momentum has been building over the last decade and has not just suddenly arrived. A lot of hard work, education, and debate have taken place during that period of time. Today, all across most western societies the issues of diversity and inclusion have become core drivers in new business thinking. In addition to the importance of making workplaces become better diverse-friendly members of society for women, BAME, LGBTQ, and other so-called "minorities," the conversation around the benefits of diversity and even the meanings of "minority" and "identity" are shifting as we speak. Even the word "minority" is beginning to lose its meaning as more understand that barriers should no longer exist. This arguably is one of the greatest generational social shifts ever. It is no longer about the male–female divide but all minority groups. Maybe one of the genuine shifts is understanding that diversity and inclusion is not a one-way process.

In past times, the conversation around diversity was often on the idea that the benefits of diversity are one-way, toward the group—traditionally female—being included. However, the hard facts have shown that diversity has been good for companies and moreover, good for the bottom line.

A 2016 report (33) from the Peterson Institute that analyzed 21,980 firms from 91 countries concluded that having more women in the senior management ranks of a company increased the profitability of a firm. Companies with 30 percent female executives, according to the report, gained as much as 6 percentage points more in profits.

For hospitality, this is important as the industry does attract many females as well as BAMEs. It does have the opportunity to take a genuine stand and be a role model for change. There is still a long way to go though.

A PWC report in 2020 (34) noted that:

Female and BAME representation at each of the most senior levels has increased—Board (up 5.3% for women/4.6% BAME),

Executive Committee (up 1.8% for women/1.4% BAME), and Direct Reports (Up 1.7% for women/1.1% BAME), demonstrating that real action has been taken at scale across the UK. If this current rate of progress continues, then the sector as a whole will reach its target of having 33% female representation across all three leadership levels by the end of 2021.

Gender equality remains a major issue in the corporate world. Despite an abundance of research confirming that companies with more women in the C-Suite are more profitable, there is, as seen, still a gender gap in the vast majority of companies. Women remain significantly underrepresented in the corporate pipeline, with fewer women than men hired at entry level, and representation declining further at every subsequent step. It is improving, it is changing, and if one wants to attract the best young talent breaking through then all companies will need to raise the bar still further. More is expected.

In all fairness, there has been a paradigm shift within corporate cultures which should see some genuine change back into reinvesting in people—including investing in employee training.

There are numerous reports emerging that showcase where females perform better than men in leadership skills. However, the danger is that the debate becomes a contest which equally is unhelpful. There needs to be a general acceptance and understanding of equality. There are many men who have become frustrated by the female support groups in leadership. It has been an important part of a process in finding equality, but the debate needs to progress and find equal inclusion for BAMEs.

We talk about all the obvious pieces in the diversity debate, gender, race, sexuality and disability but we don't talk about decision making. Leadership is about who makes the best decisions. Often this is about something deeper; introverts versus extroverts. Do we think about the risk profile of an appointment? Do we think about safe choices rather than who may bring something better and more to a role? There is a need for the discussion to think more about the diversity of the environment and how this can impact on a leader. There is a whole other level to this discussion that goes way beyond race, gender and disability. It is who is the best candidate in the circumstances.

—Kathryn Pretzel-Shiels, Consultant

The hospitality-sector is an exciting scene with a whole range of new female leaders coming to the fore as well as female chefs breaking through. The key now is for progressive-thinking companies to be looking for ways to employ and empower both more women and BAMEs within companies and in the workplace. It is no longer a moral argument; it is a proven business case.

McKinsey's most recent Delivering through Diversity report (35) found that companies that embrace gender diversity on their executive teams were more competitive and 21 percent more likely to experience above-average profitability. They also had a 27 percent likelihood of outperforming their peers on longer-term value creation. Different perspectives on customer needs, product improvements, and company well-being fuel a better business.

New Leadership to Take a Stand

As the momentum and pressure builds, so new leaders will start to emerge and they will take a stand on this issue. Together with sustainability, this is one of the major topics that the emerging generations do want to see change. Leading companies will start to show more tolerance and become strong advocates for diversity. This is again not a moral issue anymore; it is a sound business need.

The 2018 Deloitte Millennial Survey (36) shows that 74 percent of these individuals believe their organization is more innovative when it has a culture of inclusion. If businesses are looking to hire and sustain a millennial workforce, diversity must be a key part of the company culture. This 2016 survey shows that 47 percent of millennials are actively looking for diversity and inclusion when sizing up potential employers.

By the year 2025, 75 percent of the global workforce will be made up of millennials, which means this group will occupy the majority of leadership roles over the coming decade. They will be responsible for making important decisions that affect workplace cultures and people's lives.

This group has a unique perspective on diversity. While older generations tend to view diversity through the lenses of race, demographics, equality, and representation, millennials see diversity as a melding of varying experiences, different backgrounds, and individual perspectives. They view the ideal workplace as a supportive environment that gives space to varying perspectives on a given issue.

The website Socialtalent.com (37) recently highlighted Sodexo, a worldwide hospitality player, as being their No.1 lead company in diversity. They commented that:

> 40% of all staff members in Sodexo are women—that's up from just 17% in 2009. 43% of the members on the board of directors are female and the company runs 14 Gender Balance Networks worldwide. What they have found is that when there is an optimal gender balance within an organisation, employee engagement increases by 4 percentage points, gross profit increases by 23% and brand image strengthens by 5 percentage points.

In this same study, Disney came seventh and Marriott came eighth.

Procter & Gamble's (P&G) "We See Equal" Campaign (38), which was designed to fight gender bias and work toward equality for all, depicted boys and girls defying gender stereotypes. The company has a history of promoting the issue, and also records 45 percent of its managers and a third of its board as women. P&G's clear dedication to equality within its own workforce meant that the campaign came across as authentic and as a genuine push for change.

A New Era

We do live in a complex, interconnected world which is changing at speed and where diversity, shaped by globalization and technological advance, forms the base of modern society. It is understandable that there is a level of friction between generations which is further enhanced by many yearning for stronger national and local identities as many barriers are broken down.

It has been a well-trodden debate in the United Kingdom with Brexit. The gap between London and the South in its economic prosperity and the general frustration and despair felt by the Northern cities did fuel a genuine social divide. The arguments that plagued U.K. politics in 2019 were as aggressive as seen in the last 50 years. Many felt completely bemused and it did bring home how out of touch London was from the rest of the United Kingdom. For many in London, the Brexit result came as a genuine shock. London had become one of the central global centers and therefore lost sight of the fact that other regions did gain from the same prosperity. There are many communities in the North which felt almost secondary to the success of the South and did resent the many East and Central Europeans who came to the United Kingdom and took jobs. London became a fusion of cultures whilst other regions only possessed underlying tensions and resentment. It is a story which could be mirrored in many other countries and in other decades; the difference was the lack of understanding that these feelings ran as deeply as they did.

The "European" argument was centered almost on federalism, a centralist approach which would lead to better lives. However, many never desired to have their lives controlled by unelected politicians whose vision was very different to that of many who lived in the shires and counties.

It is interesting to note that just four years on, the result was almost a natural consequence as it is now clear that so many want to feel more connected to their own regions and want that separate identity which does stand apart but even today, this is a rising trend which many are just learning. Some confuse this emotion with nationalism but it is different. It was more price in localism. The world has become a tense marriage between globalization and localism living side by side.

The pace of change has been so great that it is natural that many feel lost, alienated, and even unsure. In this era of globalization, diversity in the business environment is about more than gender, race, and ethnicity. It now includes employees with diverse religious and political beliefs, education, socioeconomic backgrounds, sexual orientation, cultures, and even disabilities. In December 2019, it was noted that there are over 60 gender identities and classifications (39). It is not too surprising that many that grew up in simpler times feel bemused and confused. Even the great social and sexual revolution of the 1960s did see such freedom and openness.

Business has an important role to play and it does possess the transformative power to change and contribute to a more open, diverse, and inclusive society. At a time when many of the traditional institutions have struggled to change and adapt, many have looked toward business to play an important and meaningful role. It is for this reason that many have wanted business reasons to have been of better quality, but of course for some this has been a direct conflict with what their shareholders, owners, or business models demand. It has been a period of friction as it does take an enlightened approach to see how just all this can impact in a strong and beneficial way.

Most of us know what is right and correct. We know that equality and inclusion is the right way forward. The case grows more compelling each year and opposition naturally declines with time.

Re-Engagement

As was outlined in the previous chapter, companies are going to have to work hard in order to re-engage employees to return to the workplace or simply adapt work patterns. The desire for a better version of what existed before is stronger than ever and this does include diversity and inclusion.

What Needs to Take Place for Employers to Be Able to Effectively Engage?

Most of the leading factors are very logical and straightforward:

- *Open communication.* Everything about the modern world has been about openness and transparency. Leaders have lost trust through their lack of visibility and often being seen as inaccessible. The emerging generations expect the opposite. They want open lines of communication full of purpose and mission.
- *The work community.* This trend was most illustrated by the move toward localism. The emerging generations believe in

collaboration and cooperation between employers and also between all diverse groups of people. They do believe once again in teams more than individuals.

- *Value authenticity.* The desire and the need are for the genuine and the authentic. The days of spin no longer are effective.
- *Work that matters.* It is all about mission and purpose.
- *Be flexible.* Many millennials desire to break free from a 9-to-5 schedule. The face of the workplace is changing. There will need to be a different approach, work patterns, and balance found.

Act Bigger and Think Bigger

It was JFK who, in 1961, said the famous words "Ask not what your country can do for you but what you can do for your country" (40). Sixty years on and this is remarkably still the same ethos that sets the benchmark that many aspire to today. In today's world, leaders must excel in their work but also contribute to society; they must act bigger and think bigger than themselves.

It is ironic that this ethos possesses so much more meaning again today. It does signal the underlying call to action from the emerging generations in these chapters: a need for leaders to be bigger and act bigger than what has been seen in the last decade.

It will be a challenging time for the workplace which is going to need to adapt and change in many ways. Many of these have been highlighted earlier.

One of the growing concerns of work environments is that thinking has become far narrower due to the longer hours that many today work, having less time to reflect, the increased levels of information available, and the increased pressure on margins. However, the positive signs are this may well change with the forecast change in work patterns which are likely to emerge. The interesting challenge for the workplace is how to merge together all these major influencing factors. It does all mark a potentially major change to the past decade:

- Companies possessing stronger missions and purpose
- More focus on internal teams and communities

- A breakdown of barriers between diverse groups
- A global perspective on sustainability
- A growing focus on the local
- The importance of society and people

It is almost a full swing back in the pendulum from the past 20 years. Is this really possible? Is this change simply fool's hope?

These are the questions being discussed all across many communities and countries. Do leaders understand the challenges that lie ahead to enable them to rebuild their work cultures and business productivity? Can they reverse the falling productivity of the past decade?

It will be arguably one of the greatest challenges that leaders have faced since World War II. The difference then, of course, is that many returned home with both new skills and new aspirations to build a better world. The U.S. economy did prosper and grow. The United Kingdom built arguably its strongest social agenda of change in history.

This period will be different as although there is economic need to rebuild, the ideals and desires are different. There are many who have, in truth, enjoyed lockdown during Covid-19.

Of course, it has caused concern but it has confirmed for many their desires for greater change. The challenge for business and for leaders will be to build bridges and find a new energy to drive their companies forward.

Leaders will naturally be tested. In 2008/09, all fell back onto business models and stricter controls. The challenge in 2020/21 will be to engage and inspire, to create a new energy for the workplace to follow.

The common theme which is discussed is that of trust. Trust needs to be found once again. This will be the acid test that will separate many leaders out from others: the ability to rebuild trust with their teams. To achieve this, in fairness, they will need to mirror the desires of the millennials and meet those previously outlined desires:

- Open communication
- Visibility
- Genuine and authentic behaviors
- A belief in diversity
- A belief in progressive sustainability.

It will be a test of character for leaders who will need to adapt and change and for the strength of a culture which sits at the heart of a company.

One of the challenges today is asking aspiring leaders to be unafraid to fail so they can be better, to think more deeply and passionately about major issues, and to have principles that they are willing to make an active stand for. There is no doubting their passion for environmental and global issues, but can they be leaders?

The challenges highlighted in this book to this point are:

- The emerging generations have lost trust in leaders and in institutions.
- They believe in causes and in communities.
- They have become disengaged from the workplace.
- They lack trust in the basic intent of many businesses.
- They are led by stronger ideals which they will not compromise upon.

The challenge for today's leaders is to ensure that this generation is engaged, motivated, and empowered for their own battles in business to come. How is this to be achieved?

Of course, the answer lies in reversing the trends and barriers created over the last decade. This is the heart of the challenge. Declining trust needs to be reversed. New thinking needs to be accepted, a broader focus adopted, new leaders to be empowered.

It will be a fierce challenge but one which does need to happen so that productivity and engagement improve once again.

And in Hospitality?

Part of the preceding narrative's aim is to once again highlight the opportunity for hospitality. Hospitality should all be about community and care. The values of the emerging generations should lay the land for hospitality to prosper.

Hospitality is all about caring for others. It is about an act of service. It is also about celebrating togetherness through great food, wine, and people. It has arguably a genuine opportunity to play a bigger social role than ever.

In the workplace, food service could have a far greater and more important role to play than it ever has before. It could well be the link that does help reinforce cultures and brings people together stronger than has previously been the case. This is why leadership is so important today. It has both a social and a business role to play. It stands for something that is genuinely important in all our psyches.

In companies the role of food service could cover a number of major areas and disciplines, including:

- Excellence in health and nutrition.
- Supporting diets with new ideas and innovation.
- Bringing people together through food. Just as food has long been a social glue in society, so it can be the glue for teams within business.
- Breaking down traditional barriers.
- Creating strong service cultures which make people feel valued and wanting to interact. Creating new employee journeys which do impact on daily life.
- Combating loneliness and anxiety.

It is the same in schools where food service should aspire to:

- Support health and well-being
- Combat obesity
- Bring people together to build friendships and social cohesion
- Create positive environments which underpin culture and development
- Break down traditional barriers

Food service and hospitality has a role to play in daily life which is both social and business focused.

This particularly was well illustrated during the Coronavirus lockdown when many in hospitality did not stand idly by but volunteered to support many charitable and social initiatives. Many food service companies turned their kitchens into operations to prepare and deliver food to the vulnerable. Large exhibition centers and hotels became hospitals.

They did whatever they could, for no reward or income; they did it, and took great pride in doing so because it was, very simply, in their DNA. It did illustrate just how the industry can stand and make a difference socially as well as a business.

In May 2020, a group of leading chefs in the United Kingdom came together to create a new association, named the Ethical Chefs Association (ECA). They released a statement which noted:

> Born from a desire to help tackle the ever-more pressing issue of food poverty in the UK, The Ethical Chefs Association is being formed by a group of Hospitality Industry chefs who are coming together to raise awareness of the extent of food poverty in the UK and to unite supporters to help alleviate suffering caused by food poverty.
>
> There is genuine trust in chefs who have a passion for food and for service. There is a growing desire for Industry collaboration which this would represent. There are many who see an opportunity for genuine social change to be led by a group of great chefs from across the country who want to make a difference. This is about culinary professionals who are normally in competition, placing aside those differences, and working together towards a big picture agenda and creating necessary and positive change.
>
> This is not just another Industry body but an alliance of leading chefs who want to create an agenda for change. Food is arguably the one universal language that reaches all. It can be food, therefore, that can serve to bring people together and create a level of social change that many desire and want.
>
> As The Guardian reported, there are over 5 million families in food poverty in the UK, a situation which has been exacerbated by measures to combat Covid-19. The ECA will work to a two-pronged approach: to lobby companies within the hospitality Industry to provide support and for individual members to offer their services and chefs to support local food projects, food banks, family centres, meal distribution operations and reduce the number of families affected by hunger and lack of food.

This is not about placing any company's agenda at the forefront but ensuring that through food, the industry can help support the vulnerable in society and change lives.

Last weekend witnessed the VE Anniversary celebrations. 75 years since the end of the Second World War. It seems very apt, therefore, to launch at this time after we have faced a crisis that many have described as this generation's war. 1945–50 saw real social change with the founding of the NHS. Wouldn't be good if this was the start of a movement for chefs coming together to combat poverty? (41)

It was quite a statement. In short, it said that they did not believe that leaders would be able to collaborate well enough as they placed their own interests before a common goal. They believed that companies were simply too competitive with each other and that more could be gained through collaboration. The success of this venture is still to be seen but this does not detract from the power of the statement. Many want to see leaders begin to think bigger and act with great social compassion.

CHAPTER 6

Sustainability Through Food

On the Brink of a New Age in Sustainability and Service in Hospitality? Any discussion about hospitality and sustainability needs to have a central focus on food. Food is today's universal language. It has taken an important role in daily life. Food plays a central role in any advanced society for bringing friends together, families together, and even new relationships. It is a source of joy and experience.

However, some of the greatest threats in the field of sustainability lie in this area too. Given all this, there are three key parts to the following chapter in relation to sustainability:

1. The consumers' drive in changing how they eat and their diets
2. Food and its role in social sustainability
3. The food chain—how operators interact with suppliers

The aim of the following chapter is to try to analyze all three areas.

Change in Diets

Maybe one of the greatest changes in recent times is illustrated best by how consumers are changing their diets and thinking. In many ways, it has been a reflection of the whole sustainability process: radical development in some ways and yet only touching still the tip of the iceberg.

It is a complex landscape as it is estimated that over 50 percent today are flexitarians. There is greater education and this is motivating many to eat less meat. However, many have also turned to veganism based on ethical grounds. Many are motivated by a desire to oppose the exploitation cruelty toward animals. However, many plant-based diet followers are not necessarily vegan. Many turn to nondiary or animal products for health or dietary reasons. More and more are becoming vegan but there is also a lot of misinformation on the topic.

In the United Kingdom, the estimated number of vegans, according to The Vegan Society, stands at around 600,000 (42), which reflects an increase of 400 percent over the last four years. Some of the most famous ambassadors for the purely plant-based diet include the likes of Madonna, Benedict Cumberbatch, and even elite athletes like Venus Williams and Lewis Hamilton. However, there is still a long way to go before veganism can be viewed as a central diet as it is estimated that globally, the level of veganism only lies between 1 percent and 2 percent at most. However, the trend in the advanced economies is on the rise and for good reason:

- Vegan diets are linked to a 35 percent reduced risk of prostate cancer.
- 45 percent of the Earth's land is used for farming livestock in some way.
- As of 2018, the size of the global vegan food market was calculated to be worth $12.69 billion.
- Plant-based meat covers 2 percent of all packaged meat options.
- 38 percent of the population in India is vegetarian.
- According to the vegan statistics, more than 39 percent of people in the United States are adding more vegan food options to the dishes they eat.
- It's expected that the market for vegan meat alternatives will hit $7.5 billion globally by 2025.
- The market for baby food that's vegan or vegetarian will jump by 10.6 percent between 2016 and 2021.
- Europe represents 39 percent of the global market for meat alternatives.
- The most mainstream vegan food option is vegan junk food (43).

What Has Driven the Increase in Veganism?

A number of factors:

- Environmental effects and how for many it can play a positive personal role in combating the major challenges that the world faces. It also benefits the environment: An Oxford study has found that cutting meat and dairy from your diet has the biggest positive impact on the planet. A report in *The Guardian* commented that:

  The new research shows that without meat and dairy consumption, global farmland use could be reduced by more than 75%—an area equivalent to the US, China, European Union and Australia combined—and still feed the world.

  The new analysis shows that while meat and dairy provide just 18% of calories and 37% of protein, it uses the vast majority—83%—of farmland and produces 60% of agriculture's greenhouse gas emissions. (44)

- There is a growing consciousness over animal welfare. It serves to prevent suffering of animals forced to live under cruel circumstances.

- It is known that a plant-heavy diet has health benefits for your own body. Canada has recently massively decreased the recommended amount of dairy intake in its food pyramid.

In 2018, Just Eat noted that there had been a 987 percent increase in demand for vegetarian dishes and it classified veganism as a top consumer trend in 2018/19. Many operators have tripled the number of vegan meals that it does offer in response to this move.

This rise in attitudes is reflected in developments in the food market, as consumers' dietary trends catch the attention of the supply side. The current rise in veganism brings with itself a general interest to eat less meat. For many people, this will be one of the major decisions that they

will make during their lives. It is a very conscious move from eating traditional diets to becoming a vegan or even just a vegetarian.

Some more hard facts which do illustrate the changes taking place:

- A report by research institute Mintel found that 34 percent of
  British meat eaters have reduced their meat consumption in
  the last six months (45).
- There is an increasing number of vegan and vegetarian
  products in the market. Mintel found that between 2012 and
  2016 there was a 185 percent increase in the number of vegan
  products launched in the United Kingdom, and in 2018, it
  became the country with the most vegan products launched
  worldwide.
- The U.K. dairy milk sales decreased by £240 million between
  2014 and 2016, whilst fresh meat sales fell by £328 million
  (7.3 percent) throughout 2016. In the United States, after
  decreasing by 7 percent in 2015, milk sales are predicted to
  drop another 11 percent through 2020.

In December 2019, *EP* (46) published an article which noted that:

Just as the old saying notes "It started as a whisper and grew in
volume till one could no longer ignore it"—so it has been with the
Netflix film Game Changers: a thought provoking new film about
meat, protein and strength involving James Cameron, Arnold
Schwarzenegger, Jackie Chan, Lewis Hamilton, Novak Djokovic
and Chris Paul.

The article's writer went on to note:

Over the last week, I have encountered man after man that has lit-
erally changed their habits as a result. It was maybe best summed
up by a City Investor I was on the morning train with who noted
that he had "Subtly changed my daily habits. I am eating vegan
porridge in the morning—not great but not bad—a vegan lunch
at work but still meat on weekends. To my surprise, I reckon I am

concentrating an extra hour or so a day in just a week of changing my habits. I also reckon I have more energy which is good for my wife and kids.

This is from a former Ski Jumper and athlete. He is not alone. I reckon I have heard the same story 10x in just the last week. Can diet change the dynamic in the productivity argument?

We hosted a discussion of food trends and wellness in hotels last week and maybe one of the most telling comments was made by a senior hotel GM who noted:

It is like smoking. People knew in the 70s, smoking was bad for one's health and it took 40 years to create major change. The same is happening with diets and meat. It will be quicker, but the same process is going to happen.

So what do you believe?

If you have not made your mind up, maybe start with watching—https://gamechangersmovie.com/—I have resisted as I was being stubborn but the volume has been growing so it is only right that I do watch and reflect. (46)

Just as with sustainability, the argument for changing diets is becoming increasingly mainstream.

A few further key facts:

- The global vegan cheese market is growing at a compound annual rate of 7.7 percent and is estimated to reach $1.58 billion by 2023 in Europe alone.
- FMI's 2019 U.S. Grocery Shopper Trends report finds a rising number of households (33 percent) have at least one member voluntarily following a vegan, vegetarian, pescatarian, or flexitarian diet—a trend which is higher for Gen Z and millennial households (47).
- On the other hand, the plant-based market in the United Kingdom in 2017 was predicted by Mintel to grow by 43 percent over a four-year period.

- The U.K. meat-free market is expected to grow from £559 million in 2016 to £658 million in 2021.
- According to Allied Market Research, the global meat-substitute market is expected to have $5.8 billion sales in 2020, with an annual compound growth rate of 8.4 percent for 2015 to 2020.
- The global vegan cheese market is growing at a compound annual rate of 7.7 percent and is estimated to reach $1.58 billion by 2023 in Europe alone. Part of the reason for such tremendous growth of dairy-substitutes is lactose intolerance.

This new trend is disrupting the food market and has led to a number of major investments in new start-ups. The one which has attracted most attention is "Beyond Meat" which filed for an IPO on NASDAQ with Goldman Sachs, JP Morgan, and Credit Suisse as lead underwriters. It hasn't listed an amount that it wants to raise; in the prospectus a place-holder amount is $100 million proposed maximum aggregate offer-ing price, but this is all likely to change, notes Forbes, when investors really understand the product (48). Forbes wrote a hard-hitting piece in September 2019 which stated that:

Beyond Meat (BYND) is now probably the hottest stock in the world.

Supposedly, it tastes just like real meat but is better for animals and for the environment. Many investors expect plant-based meat to be the "next big thing." …**Soon, Every Major Food Company Will Have Its Own** Plant-Based **Burger**

These companies have deeper pockets and better distribution than Beyond Meat. They can develop new products and bring them to market much faster than Beyond Meat. Perhaps most importantly, they charge less than Beyond Meat. This will force Beyond Meat to either cut prices or surrender market share. Both would be bad for investors.

Is this perspective correct? Time will tell but there is no doubt that there is an increasing interest from both investors and consumers in such products.

The trend is not just limited to the food industry. There is a growing market for vegan fashion, where the main concern is moving away from animal skin and hair to plant-based materials like fungus textiles or recycled plant waste. This is regarded as a major trend for 2018 by Thompson Intelligence in its Future 100 Report. Likewise, beauty brands are moving toward animal-free products in the wake of this far-reaching preference shift.

The move toward veganism and vegetarianism seems to be here to stay and, looking at ongoing investments, this also seems to be what industry-leading firms think. An article in January 2020 by Lucy Wright commented that:

> Veganism is on the rise… Veganism is the subscription to a philosophy and way of living which seeks to exclude all forms of exploitation of, and cruelty to, animals for food, clothing or any other purpose; and by extension, promotes the development and use of animal-free alternatives. Whilst the animal rights movement has been, and will always remain, a crucial foundation to veganism, the growing trend toward plant-based lifestyles has, in part, been the manifestation of increased environmental awareness. (49)

There does appear to be too much evidence highlighting that change will continue and grow.

Social Sustainability Through Food

It has long been noted that food has become arguably the one true universal language: food can bring people together, break down traditional special barriers, and be a glue that does serve society. In today's society, this does play a key role. Many want to learn about the different cultures that we do live alongside each day and it is food that does reflect the history and traditions of a culture better than most. Food, therefore, has the ability to educate and teach social cohesion better than most things in the world.

It does again suggest the power that both chefs and the hospitality industry can possess if food can bring all together effectively. It has just been, too often, taken for granted. Now it needs to be actioned as it can serve to ease many social tensions.

A research project by Oxford University in 2017 (50) found that those who did eat with others are more likely to feel happy and healthy. The research noted that:

- 76 percent felt that sharing a meal was a good way of bringing people together.
- 69 percent had never eaten with their neighbors.
- 39 percent had never eaten with a community group.
- 21 percent ate their evening meal at a different time to the rest of the family.
- 1:4 of those aged over 55 noted that eating alone was a normal occurrence.

This may all seem common sense but perhaps it too is a reflection of how society in recent years has seen more people feel alone, working longer hours, and feeling stressed.

An article in *The Atlantic* (51) noted:

Sadly, Americans rarely eat together anymore. In fact, the average American eats one in every five meals in her car, one in four Americans eats at least one fast food meal every single day, and the majority of American families report eating a single meal together less than five days a week. It's a pity that so many Americans are missing out on what could be meaningful time with their loved ones, but it's even more than that. Not eating together also has quantifiably negative effects both physically and psychologically.

There is so much evidence that food/eating together creates greater understanding and greater contentment and can serve to break down barriers. If one looks at the great cities around the world from New York to San Francisco to London to Paris, migrants have played a central role in the history and development of those cities. It is something that most of us take great pride in. For many of those migrant communities, they are very aware that they have not been easily accepted and they have built bridges through food.

As communities, many have spoken about how coming together over dinner helped them build strength in adversity. Coming and "breaking bread" with their families played a crucial role in almost reassuring communities that they will be accepted and that all will be good in the end. There are many today, in the so-called majority groups, who do feel alienated and alone. Often, when one analyzes their lifestyles, they do eat alone and work long hours. Food is a social glue. Society needs to think more intelligently in how it does combat many of the major issues which are faced today, and these solutions can be supported through food.

It does all mean that hospitality has a unique power in its grasp. There is a new narrative that can be developed in this area too. Many want to fight food poverty. Many want to see traditional social tensions break down. In a time which appears full of almost constant drama, it is important that we still do all enjoy coming together and "breaking bread." It has been arguably the one constant of all the ages and still is today.

Hospitality does have a genuine opportunity to really stand tall and have a social impact that does really play a positive role across communities, in schools, and in workplaces. It is not just in breaking down the barriers in communities but also in educating the young about the importance of fresh food and in combating obesity.

It was this challenge that stood behind EP's own launch of a campaign entitled "Fuelling Productivity" (52) in the United Kingdom. The aim was to make a strong case that food can truly impact on productivity and welfare in companies, in schools, in society as a whole. Too often companies have focused on their business models rather than just on how great food can make a real difference. The campaign did serve to bring together over 30 major companies. In January 2020, EP published the following article (52):

The food service sector is at the forefront of the battle to combat obesity, poor nutrition and mental health in the young.

There is increasing acceptance that the need to nurture the young is not simply confined to education; in fact, it includes everything that surrounds the entire system. Schools have been working hard to create new solutions which aim to support young people in daily life. This includes helping to create new processes that develop mental robustness, strong life skills and a greater understanding of good diet and nutrition. There is a genuine enthusiasm and demand for change, as well as for the need to ensure young people are being nurtured as effectively as possible.

The foodservice sector sits right at the centre of this drive, and companies are becoming increasingly aware that their remit can be far wider reaching than has traditionally been the case. Foodservice today really does impact directly on diet and nutrition, and it is an important ally in combating both obesity and mental health issues. Indeed, schools and educational establishments all over the country are reintroducing cookery lessons back into the school curriculum in order to teach important life skills alongside the benefits of effective teamwork.

We believe that this in itself could herald the start of a new golden era for foodservice, one in which it plays an ever-higher profile role in daily life. Food is one of the few genuine universal languages today; it brings people together and fosters a genuine sense of joy in daily life. We believe in the power, importance and influence of foodservice, and that it really can play an important role in everyday life. There are great people all across the sector who want to create special experiences while making a real difference. Foodservice is currently engineering its own change agenda; one whose story we are keen to tell. Please, we ask, do come and join us in this journey.

The Food Chain

At the start of this section, it is important to highlight the work of David Read, Chairman of Prestige Purchasing (53), who has been a powerful advocate for the need for genuine change in the food cycles. He has been a passionate advocate for the need of change in the four core areas noted as follows.

The food chain/cycle has been the focal point for many discussions in relation to sustainability. With the market under pressure, there will be an ever greater need for operators to collaborate with their suppliers in order to deliver improvements.

There are four core areas which need to be considered most:

- Deforestation
- Renewables
- Transport
- Waste

These four areas have seen greater levels and intensity of focus which do provide the foundations for future progress.

Deforestation

Many understand that the issue of deforestation has long been a major concern for the environment. To outline the scale of the issue, a couple of initial facts are to be considered:

- In 2018, 8.5 million acres of virgin rainforest was cut down globally.
- About 9,762 km^2 (3,769 square miles) of rainforest was lost for 12 months through July 2019, according to the release from The National Institute for Space Research (INPE). That's a 29.5 percent increase over the previous 12 months (54).

As will be well known, forests, especially tropical forests, store enormous amounts of carbon. When forests are destroyed, that carbon is released to the atmosphere, accelerating global warming. In addition to storing carbon, forests provide important habitat for a long list of endangered species, and they offer many other benefits, such as clean water, forest products, and livelihoods for indigenous communities.

With large areas of cheap land, relatively low labor costs, and a year-round growing season, the tropics have become a favored location for large-scale industrial commodity production. Eliminating emissions from commodity-driven tropical deforestation can play a huge role in reducing climate change. Clearing forests to grow crops such as palm oil and soy or to raise cattle is thought to be responsible for up to 15 percent of total global greenhouse gas emissions.

The obvious starting point for forest destruction is logging. What generally happens is that timber generally used for construction or high-end products like furniture is harvested and the rest is left. These degraded forests are then targeted for conversion to food production.

Just four commodities are the largest drivers of tropical deforestation:

- *Beef*
  Of the four major deforestation drivers, converting forest to pasture for beef (largely in Latin America) has by far the largest impact. Mercosur nations (the Southern Common Market) are all to some extent involved in deforestation, with the highest levels in Brazil and Paraguay, and perhaps less so in Uruguay. This is a relatively simple problem to solve.
- Soy
  Growing global demand for meat and dairy products has contributed to the doubling of soybean production in the last 20 years. Soy is primarily used to feed pork, poultry, and cattle, though significant amounts are also used to produce vegetable oil and biodiesel. Large soybean fields in the tropics, particularly in Latin America, are often planted on newly deforested land. There is an organization called RTRS (Round Table on Responsible Soy) which certifies sustainable soy production. Their certification assures that soy, either as a raw material or as a by-product, originated from a process that is environmentally correct (including deforestation), socially adequate, and economically viable.
- Palm oil
  Because of its neutral flavor and aroma and great cooking properties, palm oil is incredibly useful and versatile. It's an attractive crop because it's so efficient to grow. One can get at least two times more palm oil per acre than other vegetable oils and sometimes up to 10 times more. As demand for palm oil has soared, huge areas of tropical rainforest and peat land in South East Asia were cleared to expand small holdings and make way for large-scale plantations.

Like soy it is possible to try to ensure that products containing palm oil have sustainable certification—in this case RSPO (Round Table on Sustainable Palm Oil).

Both the RSPO and RTRS have been the subject of some criticism for their slow pace of progress but they remain the best tool we have right now to place pressure back up the supply chain.

- Coffee and tea

The product naturally grows in tropical countries near the equator, such as Indonesia, Brazil, India and Uganda.

Production, particularly in the coffee market, is undertaken by thousands of small-scale producers. In the light of increasing global demand, many farmers are expanding their fields by felling trees in these forests and burning the dense underbrush, using chemical herbicides to control weeds. This is particularly distressing as often there are opportunities for them to manage yields more effectively through organic means, creating less pressure to grab more land.

Climate change is also impacting where coffee and tea can be grown. Coffee is sensitive to temperature change, so there is a huge amount of work going on currently to try to develop strains that are more tolerant of change. If we are unable to see success in this, then it may result in significantly more deforestation in years to come as plantations migrate uphill to find more temperate conditions.

Renewables

Rightly, there has been a huge amount of attention paid in the past two years to plastics.

"Single-use" was declared word of the year by *Collins Dictionary* in 2018. The biggest focus in food service on plastics is within the food and drink "to go" market which is worth around £22 billion. This is a major problem to replace but progress has been made. It has become a common principle already for those keen to tackle plastics to use the Rethink/Reduce/Rese/Recycle model.

- Rethink: Does the product need to be packaged at all? Or can it be packaged with nonplastic?

- Reduce: Can the product be packaged less? Or can the product be replaced?
- Reuse: an the packaging be used again?
- Recycle: Can the packaging be recycled?

There has been substantial innovation which has come to the fore, particularly in compostables. Pret A Manger witnessed a 10-fold increase in customers bringing in their own cups after increasing its beverage discount from 25 percent to 50 percent in January 2018. At the end of 2019, the retail operator served more than 100,000 drinks in reusable cups each week.

Transport

People often quote "Food Miles" as being a sole determinant on distribution. But like most things, it is a more complex issue than a simple cause. It just requires more considered strategies in a number of key areas:

- Ranging
  Can an origin that is closer be found? How critical is it that an operator buy products that have to travel significant distances? How much of what is bought travels by air? How much of this is truly understood?
- Frequency
  How frequently are deliveries really needed? Have habits become lazy? Could storage be increased?
- Consolidation
  How can distribution be made more effective?
- Production impact

How does one understand the impact of productions?
These are all valid questions and issues that do need far greater understanding.

Waste

Waste has come to the fore as an issue in the last few years. Huge volumes of waste are generated in the food service/hospitality sector every year, of which:

- 1.5 m tons are sent for disposal.
- 0.6 m tons (41 percent) is food waste.
- 0.4 m tons is avoidable food waste.

It is believed that the cost of avoidable food waste is almost £1 for every meal produced. Rates of composting and food going to anaerobic digestion are reported to be very low. On average, food waste initiatives in food service create a 14:1 return on investment.

It's ironic that an area that has such a strong financial return should receive relatively little attention at this time. Again, it is an area for education. It is also a cost to retrain operators to act and behave differently.

Supplier Management

Marks & Spencer have become something of a benchmark in their involvement and management of suppliers to raise the bar on their own sustainability performance. They use a simple sustainability ladder built to measure their supplier commitments to Marks & Spencer's plan.

Suppliers are rated by:

- Environment
- Ethical trade
- Lean manufacturing

They are then ranked according to performance as follows:

- Provisional
- Bronze
- Sliver
- Gold

Suppliers are rewarded for progressing up the ladder and can use their Marks & Spencer's status in their promotional and marketing streams.

The industry is able to make a difference to the environment, and in fairness, it is making great strides in achieving progress, though progress has just been slow. All the aforementioned are well-known and well-accepted facts for close to 10 years and yet it has only been since 2016 to 2017 that real action has begun to really take place.

It is interesting how much of the sustainability story follows the same trend, even if in different fields. Awareness of these issues has been known but action was only truly initiated during the mid-2010 to 2020 decade. It is now in the next decade that real action will take place.

CHAPTER 7

The Cousins—Sustainability and Service

The relationship between service and sustainable business has rarely been explored but the two are closely connected. They are like cousins, not quite in the same family but closely related. If a focus of any CEO or MD is on developing a strong, sustainable business then this logically requires a strong service ethic which will sit at the core of how a business interacts with customers and which builds loyalty and trust. It also requires great people who are positively engaged in the business and interacting with the external audience.

As has been highlighted throughout this book, the emerging generations place a genuine importance on people once again: in communities and in companies. Service is one of the very few skills which can really make a person feel valued, feel special.

Service enhancement will play a central role in support of the sustainability argument. It will be services that engage customers and how these evolve will underpin the success of hospitality's progress on a bigger level.

We have written on the need for leaders to adapt and change, for business too is far broader in perspective and to change. However, these changes can simply not happen without real change taking place in how the business also engages on the front line with customers and clients. Real change can only, in truth, really take place if customers and clients feel more valued. They then naturally support the change that needs to take place and ensure that business performance is strong.

At the end of the day, all leadership teams may have a whole set of new pressures to face but results are needed in order to keep all sides supportive. It is a remarkably tough challenge for leaders to reverse all the faults of the last decade and create a new balance which keeps investors, shareholders, employees, and customers fully engaged with renewed missions. It is service that creates the real momentum for change.

Leaders are being asked to embrace a purpose beyond themselves and the immediate pressures. It is logical to argue that if a business can develop a stronger "fan" base, then of course, results are able to stay strong as a business platform is developed. However, creating the fan base requires a service ethic that really can impact on the customer to a level beyond others.

It has been an interesting swing in time as in the 1990s, service really did have a dominant theme. Founded in 1965 (55), TGI Fridays engaged a strong customer-friendly theme as the founder, Alan Stillman, wanted the restaurant to be equally appealing to women as much as men. He believed in the base principle that men would follow venues where women were. However, the ethos was deeper and focused too on creating a new experience for the customer. The employees were young and wore red-and-white-striped soccer shirts, and every time someone had a birthday, the entire restaurant crew came around with a cake and sang TGI Fridays' traditional birthday song. It is old hat now but at the time was groundbreaking. It placed the customer first and generated a different psychology between guest and employee.

Disney possessed a strong mantra which was focused on exceeding the expectations of all those that came to their parks or watched their films. Walt Disney is famed for once remarking that:

> Whatever you do, do it well. Do it so well that when people see you do it, they will want to come back and see you do it again, and they will want to bring others and show them how well you do what you do. (56)

It was Disney in the 1990s that "sparked" a new focus on service with a strong narrative that openly outlined how they expected all their employees to constantly exceed expectations and find ways of creating a wow factor in service. Employees were rewarded by the feedback of customers believing that their expectations had been exceeded. At that time, Disney argued that it was the smallest details that create the wow factor and often, as an example, cited the film "Who Framed Roger Rabbit."

They would show a scene where Bob Hoskins would be fighting with Roger Rabbit and the illustrations would not just accurately feature how a ceiling light would move after being hit but also its shadow. Although no viewer would consciously see the detail of the shadow, it was this level of detail that would set Disney apart. This philosophy followed them into their theme parks where each park has an underground village beneath. This was to ensure that the actors/characters would never need to "leave character" or scene and could easily travel beneath the park in order to take a break. It was important to Disney, for example, that Winnie the Pooh would not suddenly be seen out of place.

Little has changed with Disney's mantra from the day it was founded to today. Even today Disney believe that "Today, companies compete as much on customer experience as they do on product and price" (56). They believe in three core planks in achieving this goal:

1. Create a common purpose for the organization.
2. Understand your customer holistically: a need to understand the customer beyond traditional boundaries.
3. View exceptional service as an economic asset rather than as a cost.

Many experts today argue that a successful company must have a message at its core which is genuine and authentic: possess a mission that the customer understands and is engaged by. Service is key to this. The retail chain Pret a Manger really raised the bar in how customers were served and were rewarded with greater loyalty. Their customer ethos was almost unmatched on the High Street.

Service leadership should be focused on an overall mission in how can it inspire and serve others through actions. There are many examples of brands who have been seen as self-serving organizations, driven strictly by profitability, which have exceeded the expectations of their shareholders. However, to create a truly activate strategy and transform organizations, a sense of broader purpose and service should be part of the equation. Although the bottom line is a fundamental in all business, it is people's desire to make a contribution which is more meaningful, sustainable, and enduring.

The Power of SMEPS

It all links together in a chain: *service, mission, employee engagement, productivity, and sustainability (SMEPS)*. This is the central plank. The challenge is for it to become central to the thinking of hospitality leaders in their strategies.

It does mark a significant change to the strategies of the last decade, which has seen all these areas decline. It is fair to argue that the increased focus on profitability and shareholder return has seen less emphasis on mission and service as well as employee engagement. Productivity has become a major concern. All these areas of focus are what both the fast emerging generations desire and what the largest group of consumers also want. The desire for higher standards and change does reflect the thinking and desire of the new emerging generations who want to be valued as individuals, possess a strong global conscience, as well as have an eye on the long term. It is natural that this concept of SMEPS should sit at the heart of all hospitality strategies.

It is significant change which is needed but it is not any revolution or transformation—more a renewal of values which did used to sit at the heart of the industry. It is far more about creating straightforward and solid steps to change. At the heart of the discussion to follow lies a core concept that suggests that operations need to possess a customer-friendly approach that creates genuine experiences that make the guest feel valued and confident.

To achieve this requires two central planks.

1. An operation whose approach reflects the desires and aspirations of the guests.
2. The ability to connect with each guest. Many in industry have one of two views that govern how they behave. First, many view the guest as entering their premises, their homes, and their role is to host the guest and it is for the guest to follow their rules. The second see that their role is to enter the guest's lives, that they are the guest and their role is to ensure that they enrich the guest's stay.

The industry is truly world-class and is made up of a great variety of operations from the chef patron restaurant to the country hotel, the major

city center destination to beach resorts to nightclubs, casinos, casual dining, branded operations, and beyond. The two core common denomina-
tors are essentially how they make a guest feel and if the operation appeals
to their own aspirations. It is a deeper and more complex subject that
many realize but also simple at the same time. How do you create a strong
connection with a guest? How can you exceed their expectations?

The world today asks a whole new set of questions. It can no longer
just be about words but needs to be about progressive and proactive deeds
and actions. It is an exciting period of time as many hotels are seeking
to create new levels of service experiences. As examples of some recently
quoted include:

- There are hotels who will discover a guest's dietary requirements and create a personalized menu for the guest, with the
  bespoke menu placed in the guest's room on arrival.
- Some hotels will research the guest on social media and
  download photos and place them in picture frames in the
  guest's room in order to make the room feel like a home away
  from home.
- Some hotels research the guest's favorite soft drinks and will
  greet the guest on arrival, at the door, with a glass of their
  favorite.
- In the same way, research into a guest can tell the hotel of a
  guest's hobbies and a simple gift, related to a key passion of
  the guest, can create a memorable wow factor for the guest.
- One of the trends in focus is how to create a memory for the
  guest which will create a lasting impression and loyalty. Of
  course, this is rarely a major gesture but a moment of genuine
  great service which does exceed any expectation.

Service is one of the simplest of roles and yet maybe one of the hardest
to do in order to be exceptional. Hospitality is about being hospitable and
caring for the well-being of others. It is about creating experiences that
do make guests feel safe and create either an escape from daily life or an
environment that a guest wants to experience again. Talk to anyone in any
walk of life and they will recall, with a smile, a great culinary experience,

a memorable night in a hotel, a special moment of shared love in a restaurant or hotel, or even a great evening with friends spent together. Hospitality is the framework that does create lasting memories.

Hospitality is about service and care for others and this will be needed more than ever as we move forward.

Empathy at Its Heart

It is an old saying that "anyone who enters hospitality must have a love of people and a desire to make people happy." It does sit at the very core of hospitality. Many industry leaders have compared the role of hospitality to that of a theater where the employees are like actors/actresses whose role is to bring satisfaction to their visiting guests.

It has played a central social role for all the ages. The industry just has not often made the most of the argument. It has waited for others to argue the case.

Many customers seek greater experiences, ones which are almost personalized and unique. Then there is a strong argument that service will once again be of ever greater importance: that many people will value those that do offer real care and are prepared to go the extra mile. This is not just in hospitality but across all disciplines.

In recent times, most have become weary of call centers and centralized processes which offer little human interaction or care, if any, and call assistants who are often patronizing, arrogant, and aloof.

There have been so many comments over the hope that a real service ethic emerges once again and that companies move away from their own internal agendas dominating a process and rather become focused on the client or customer. The hope is also that this period will see the end of lazy service. There are no few clients who wonder if their service providers are the ones providing the service or whether it has been the other way round.

Service is one of the greatest skills and, too often, the impact that it is able to have on a person's psychology and day is underestimated. Great service is of course about detail and also about care/empathy. AI does have a place as together they do create a powerful combination. It is the role of leaders to inspire teams to provide service that can make a difference to a guest's day.

Many guests enjoy service for the personal connection that it provides them. There is a great story of a person that travelled 20 miles each day into London just for the way one London café made his morning coffee and the service they offered. He noted:

> They always made me feel welcome and as though I was the most important person to enter their café every day. That was worth the hour's journey to go there and another hour back again. The Journey cost me more than the coffee but who cares—I felt bloody great. (57)

In a world where trust has become such a major issue, it can be service that creates the basis for trust to be found. Marco Truffelli, former MD with Rocco Forte Hotels, noted in an article for *EP magazine* (58):

> It is easy often to see and feel great service as compared to the "transactional" moment when all that the person cares about is the bill being paid. We have all directly experienced transactional behaviours: moments such as when the receptionist does not look up from her computer to even acknowledge your presence or the times, we are left waiting at a table to place an order. Maybe even that moment when, caught in a sudden downpour, and finding oneself drenched and feeling sorry for oneself, the doorman asks "how is your day?" as they look more concerned at the puddle that you may bring into the hotel or restaurant.
>
> How do you make that person feel that you have the situation under control, that they are cared for and need not be concerned?
>
> How many times have you arrived late at a hotel, only to find that there is no more room service for the evening? Could the hotel do something to earn your gratitude and loyalty? How could they exceed expectations?

As Michael Gray, a former VP for Hyatt in London, noted:

> The real change in mind-set is when you stop seeing a guest as entering your space but that you are entering their lives and stories. What can you do to enhance your role and place in that story?

It does all tie back to the debate on visible leadership. How do you ensure that your team is prepared to do something exceptional that will create a lasting impression and a loyalty from the customer that may, over time, be worth many thousands in income? One definition of hospitality is the "friendly and generous treatment of guests" but is this a good enough definition? Is friendly and generous the same as empathetic and caring?

During the covid lockdown, many did watch with both pride and pleasure at how so many hospitality professionals, all across the world, did great work, delivering food to the vulnerable for absolutely no reward at all no money, often not even a "thank you" as the food is delivered outside, subject to social distancing regulations. They were doing their part to help combat the virus and still most importantly, to serve.

It says so much for those that work in the industry as altruism is driven by empathy.

Marco Truffelli again remarked, in the early stages of the covid lockdown period (58):

> It is hard for Italy at this time as the country is so used to being loved and being a top destination for visitors. It is in our own soul to care to those that visit the great country.

I still remember vividly a BBC Radio caller complaining about the overly extensive coverage of the Japanese earthquake and tsunami in 2011, and asking the radio presenter how many times the BBC would continue to interrupt our lives and repeat the 'same news' about the death toll over and over again.

While a few weeks ahead of the Covid-19's international developments, with my native home country being the first hit in Europe, I found that the daily narrative in my adoptive home country was somehow distant and, to a degree, relatively unsympathetic (one 'celebrity doctor' even suggesting that the Italian lock-down was just an excuse for a long siesta), and, yet, once the nasty wave reached and trespassed our borders, the public, in truly British fashion, rallied behind the NHS and the front-line workers and embraced a national code of empathy display. The 8pm claps being a beautiful and moving example of such emotional demonstration.

The real danger is that, while the death toll continues to increase close to our homes, in parallel, personal economic and social hardship spreads exponentially and people's ability to genuinely empathise with the wider loss of life is challenged at its core. I have witnessed many reactions to the daily 'statistics' and from shock, fear and horror, in a relatively short period of time, we have moved to increase numbness, rapidly changing to a predominant desensitisation. As hospitality professionals, we have a duty to share our predominantly innate care and genuine feeling for 'the other' and help fellow human beings to acquire a greater sense of empathy.

How do we do it? Let's share the benefits of demonstrating empathy, how to recognise emotions in others, how to feel those emotions and how to suitably comment on them. Let's be the role model by showing empathy in response to something somebody else has done or shared. Then we can practice at showing empathy. Finally, just like train the trainer, we can provide constructive feedback on efforts in showing empathy: either praise when someone has reacted appropriately or constructively provide feedback on how better to assess the emotion of another person or response to a specific emotion. Indeed, as the Coronavirus furlough scheme encourages time for training, why not using this opportunity to provide life and professional training on how to be more empathetic?

As the Ritz-Carlton's brand promise "Ladies and Gentlemen Serving Ladies and Gentlemen", in its simplicity, is still guiding many of our ethos of hospitality, we can practice a very human innate feeling of being "*People caring for People*" (58).

It is Not Easy to Ensure that Service is Genuine

There are many articles and books which will say that the secret to great service is to love your customers, serve them unconditionally and to win their hearts. This is all true but as the old saying goes "it is not what you say, it is how you say it". There is a big difference between saying the right words and acting them through genuine and often proactively unexpected behaviours.

How does one create the difference? How does one ensure that teams can act with freedom and with real care? This is where leadership is so important as it does stem from the behaviours and actions of the leader. The challenge is to create the right culture so that the culture almost becomes an invisible manager. It is a belief in something "of value" that does serve to bring people together and a belief in something bigger to. Good cultures cannot exist if the core pillars are not in place—trust, safety, and belief—trust in the leadership team; feeling safe to be able to express oneself and take a risk and belief in what the company is striving to achieve.

The Power of Service in Building a Sustainable Business

Service plays an important role today as it can serve to break down barriers and help many find a new purpose. It is often surprising and interesting to see just how many people today want a mission which does help others. Of course, this has been enhanced during the Covid-19 crisis but already existed as a growing theme amongst the millennial generations. It is almost as though the last decade has seen a complete pendulum movement as it was not very long ago that many were arguing that the drive of self-interest had long become a prevalent dimension of everyday life. The trend had been toward self-interest, materialism, and competitive aggression, and had had substantial column inches dedicated to it over the past 20 years. For a whole variety of reasons there has been a shift in cultural emphasis from "we are in this together" to the growing culture of "me." As was outlined in the opening chapter to this book, this trend and focus had arguably grown stronger over the last decade since the great crash of 2008/09. However, it seems to have swung back without some almost noticing.

Many point toward social media as heightening the emphasis of the importance of the self and one can see that many journalists have moved from being commentators and observers to viewing themselves as modern "Bernstein's and Woodward's," all out to break the story or be the voice that people listen to. One can argue that the media has been losing the trust of many at the same rate that the egos of some reporters have grown.

There is some truth in this argument, but it also has more to do with the 24/7 nature of today's media which creates a constant pressure on having engaging stories to tell. It will naturally create intense bubbles around any real story and also drama over the most mundane of story. Loss of trust is natural if drama is created from a low base. Most audiences want to be entertained but also be able to access objective, informed perspectives. This used to be the role of the major newspapers but of course, with the advent of the Internet and 24/7 news channels, the dynamics have naturally changed.

It is the same with business. Business is expected to perform strongly, consistently, and with very little space for error or mistake. It all creates a naturally stressful pressure cooker, so how can this be adjusted in a sensible manner which allows new philosophies to emerge and grow?

Many have been arguing that self-interest will always jeopardize long-term organizational progress and strategy. If self-interest lies at the heart, then so does rhetoric with little supporting action. This naturally hinders real progress in numerous areas and serves to alienate both internal and external audiences.

At the time of writing, many believe and hope that the Covid-19 crisis does serve to create a genuine change in how people view daily life and the world. Is it a coincidence that the "Black Lives Matter" movement evolved to another level during this period? The movement has existed and has been growing for a number of years but the *New York Times* noted that in May and early June 2020 (59), support for the movement doubled. It became a dominant theme in the United Kingdom too and became one of the leading stories.

The *New York Times* noted (59) that:

Perhaps most significant, the Civiqs data is not alone in suggesting that an outright majority of Americans agree with the central arguments of Black Lives Matter.

A Monmouth University poll (60) found that 76 percent of Americans consider racism and discrimination a "big problem," up 26 points from 2015. The poll found that 57 percent of voters thought the anger behind the demonstrations was fully justified, while a further 21 percent called it somewhat justified.

Polls show that a majority of Americans believe that the police are more likely to use deadly force against African Americans, and that there's a lot of discrimination against black Americans in society. Back in 2013, when Black Lives Matter began, a majority of voters disagreed with all of these statements.

It does highlight the broader change in thinking that is taking place across many societies at this time.

So How Can Real Change Be Achieved?

It is the old saying that a movement is created when the many see the reason for it. Martha Graham commented that (61): "All that is important is this one moment in movement. Make the moment important, vital, and worth living. Do not let it slip away unnoticed and unused."

The demand for change is growing as a new generation with new values and beliefs emerges. Each generation naturally creates change and it is happening again.

At the heart lies a desire to create a genuine purpose in business which is bigger than just the immediate. This has long been a major discussion as many operating models have become too dominated by the desire for more immediate returns. However, a sustainable business model is about being more than a focus on quarterly reports. It is about building a business that serves the shareholders, the employees, society, and the environment. This is the objective that so many want to see. It will not be easy to achieve, it will have setbacks but it is the rising aspiration of many.

For hospitality, there is already a social role which it can play if it so desires. It can lead and provide a service in communities, across all communities and society.

It has played a central social role for all the ages. The Coffee Houses of the 1700s dominated in the great old cities. Then the Gentleman's clubs and the local pubs. The great old Nightclubs of the wartimes brought much escape and solace from the sadness of war. Even in modern times, the leading sitcom of the 1980s—"Cheers"—was based in a bar and the one of the 1990s—"Friends"—in a coffee house.

Hospitality is central in society and has its role to play. The industry just has not often made the most of the argument.

The Purpose of Leaders

Most leaders will naturally express a desire to build a long-term sustainable business. For many it is, of course, about wealth creation but most will also have an eye on their legacy. Any leader will know that they will be defined by how the business is viewed and performs over a period of time. A legacy is achieved through good performance year after year.

It is therefore understandable that most will want to create, serve, build, and improve in the service of a broader and more long-term goal.

It is this sense of meaningful contribution which is the reason people get satisfaction out of mentoring and teaching others. However, many leaders suppress this desire in order to serve more practical, short-term objectives. People want to serve others, but for many reasons often end up serving only their own more immediate agenda.

For a company to build a strong, long-term business in hospitality, the power of service does need to sit at the heart. After all it does sit at the heart of the natural psychology that many within hospitality do possess. However, it goes well beyond hospitality and can impact on any business. Leadership development, after all, is meant to improve how executives serve their teams, their customers, their organizations, and themselves. However, far too many people have been conditioned to take care of themselves first, whether for survival, financial reward, or an ego boost. The pendulum must swing in the other direction. Leaders need to experience the power of selfless service and of subjugating one's own needs to a larger purpose.

When combined, purpose and service are the fuel for transformation. As Winston Churchill said, "If the human race wishes to have a prolonged and indefinite period of material prosperity, they have only got to behave in a peaceful and helpful way toward one another" (62). Service to others is more than just a nice thing to do. It inspires deep, lasting change and of course, a legacy.

Success does not just happen; it comes from hard work and from growth through learning. In the ideal world, cultures that possess purpose also teach character, not success. but how to respond to setbacks and believe in a mission. Service is a mission and can play such an influential role in lives.

It must however be based on actions rather than words. Consider for a moment a culture that is truly focused on character: humility, service, and kindness and then another which aims to be process-led, efficient, and convenient. We have all experienced both, but which leaves you with a memory and a desire? One is based on the heart of the business while the other is based on the mechanics of the business.

In fairness, both have their place. The first at the top end of the industry. The second with supermarkets and fast food restaurants. There are many successful millionaires who have owned fast food franchises and will not hear a word against their systems.

McDonalds' is arguably one of the great restaurant groups the world has ever known. It is hard to argue against their success. They have a reputation as having the best systems and the best training. Their health and safety is first class. It serves over 69 million customers each day in over 100 countries. Its success is based on process and systems and it has worked highly effectively.

However, for restaurants that offer great skilled service the process is different. It starts with the leadership and flows up through the team to the guests. No one can expect a team to live out the spirit of hospitality in service of others if the culture and leadership teams do not walk the talk ourselves. It goes back to the Disney example; it is all modeled through everyone striving each day to achieve excellence, together.

Training and Development

One of the most controversial areas has been the amount invested in training and development. There are many organizations who will argue that great service can only be delivered through a strong training program and yet across industries, training budgets have been shown to have been halved over the last decade. Many argue this is relative as much training has moved online which appeals to younger generations and there is a partial truth in this argument. However, history will show that long-term continuous success often has a strong training culture at its heart.

Great service does need training as do all disciplines that require a strong individual professional performance. Sports players train five days per week in order to excel. The Military train each day. Doctors, lawyers, and accountants spend years training and continuing to train in their disciplines, so it is logical that great service too often requires intense and continuous periods of understanding and learning. Training and learning create not just purpose, but the confidence to be able to deliver when the pressure is high. If one instills purpose and empathy at the core, then it will naturally begin to start building a growing tribe of engaged customers.

Leadership plays a common and important purpose in building teams:

- Without vision, people do not know what they're supposed to aim for. What's our common goal? What do we want to achieve in business? What is our business philosophy? What makes us different to anyone else?

- Without understanding excellence, the team cannot understand their purpose and objective. Marco Truffelli, a leading hotelier across Europe, earlier referred to The Ritz Carlton and their philosophy. At the start of their day, the Ritz Carlton teams gather for their daily line up. During this 15-minute gathering, they do three things. They hear what is happening at a corporate level and what is happening at the local hotel, such as a memorable story of how putting their vision to work has affected a guest. They also review their 20 core values. These values are always within the team members' sight and hearing. There is never an excuse for the team members to not know how to respond in any given situation in order to accomplish the Ritz Carlton Golden Standard of Service. They are ladies and gentlemen serving ladies and gentlemen.

Another example is Taylors of Harrogate who oversee Yorkshire Tea, the famous Bettys Team Rooms ,as well as a number of other businesses. It may have changed but back in the late 2000s, they had a philosophy of making sure that their teams meet, but the meetings could only be two minutes long. It ensured that the leaders of each team had to be prepared and needed to keep their communication short and to the point. At the same time, it improved interaction as all would listen intently for two minutes and so it set a tone for action over words.

A similar philosophy had been introduced by ASDA's former CEO, Archie Norman, who used to have a room with tables but no chairs next to his office. His view was that if someone could not sit down, they would not waffle and waste time. It sent out a message and sat at the heart of a culture that in turn became very successful.

When recruiting it is important that all buy into the mission and the objectives being set. Disney again excelled in this area and all new recruits are asked to watch a film in advance of interviews which set out expectations very clearly. It also sets out the standards the company strives for.

The outcome of training and development of front-line crew members should reflect the values of the owners.

- It is also important that employees know and understand their purpose in their position. The goal is to provide a seamless delivery of our product or service. For that to happen, each team member needs to know what they're responsible for and how to best serve in that position. This can only be achieved through communication.

Empathy

Empathy does sit at the heart of hospitality. Arguably it is the most important personality trait that someone in hospitality may possess.

There is another old saying that "people don't care how much you know until they know how much you care".

It is true. Adam Elliott (Founder of Paragon Hospitality) noted that:

The leaders that you remember in your career, are the ones that lived life with conviction and with passion. I love working with passion, with those who care and then I have all the time in the world for them. If they talk to me in clichés and with corporate language, I soon switch off.

In hospitality, people do need to know that it is all genuine. A director who used to work for Adam Elliott fondly recalled the first time they met:

Adam listened to me for about ten minutes before telling me that I was talking rubbish. We proceeded to have a row—but I loved him for his honesty and genuine approach. It made me want to work for him. We may not have agreed but I knew I could work for this man.

Of course, the issue is far deeper than just being genuine and authentic. The key part of the previous information was that both parties showed they cared, were human, and could understand each other. With empathy, the key is to be able to understand how someone feels. We need to be able to read a difficult situation. We need to understand vulnerability, fear, and distress and be able to act accordingly. We need to be able to place ourselves away and focus on the other person. This does take some courage and a genuineness and selflessness of heart to help another. For some it is natural. For others it needs to be trained through teaching and experience.

No one wants to be judged for their failings. No one wants to feel as though they have failed. Can you then place your arm around another, reassure them in the darkness of their moment, that all will be fine and not to worry? Are you able to take on their fear and ease it?

The knowledge that a leader cares about your concerns builds trust.

There is a story told about a guest who called the hotel general manager to the room where he was staying to complain that some very important documents had been thrown away by the housekeepers who had cleaned his room. The client was of great importance, so he sent a team down to the local rubbish tip to search for the papers. After hours of searching, they managed to locate the papers, but they had been stained and not for use. The general manger though was very proud of his team who had searched for hours through rubbish just to find the guest's missing papers. It showed real character and desire to help the guest. As it turned out, the guest was not as concerned as he had a spare set of papers but appreciated the efforts taken by the hotel.

Another more amorous story was of a general manager who used to tease his head chef over a crush that he had on a waitress. One evening whilst checking the hotel was all closed down for the evening, he wandered into the kitchen where he found his chef in a romantic moment with the waitress. The general manager simply smiled and said, "Goodnight Chef" and left them together.

Then there is a story of a general manager who watched on as one of his junior female event organizers was heavily criticized by a client who was being unreasonable and demanding. The criticism left the event managers deeply upset for having let the client down. As she arrived home, there was a bouquet of flowers awaiting her from the general manager with the simple message that "We may fail today but tomorrow is a new day where we may soar."

Business is business. It will have its high moments and its low. However, empathy is about placing a person first and understanding but also meeting their needs. It is a very special skill which makes many in hospitality stand apart. When greeting a guest, one needs to greet them as a person first and their business as secondary. Service is about how we make an individual feel at a moment in time. If we excel, more business will naturally follow.

During any career in hospitality one will see anger, tears, sadness, despair, and sorrow. None are positive emotions, but all need to be faced. In the majority of cases, most people just want to be faced by an example of kindness and compassion. There is always something that can be said to show that person, however bad they may feel, that they do matter and are important.

This is why putting others before ourselves at all times is so incredibly important in the spirit of hospitality. It doesn't matter how ridiculous their request may sound; it doesn't matter whether company policy allows for the required response. What matters is making the guest feel important enough for someone to empathize with their felt need and work with them to meet it.

London Edition Hotels often talked of how they empowered their Room Service teams to spend as was needed to resolve a complaint. As this policy was launched, there was some concern that costs could escalate but instead they found that their teams responded with greater care, spending less and gaining greater levels of satisfaction. It showed that things are not always about cost but also about trust.

If one wants to be a leader in a hospitality environment, then it is about thinking and serving people. It may sound like a strange comment, but the vast majority of people are neither comfortable in themselves nor relaxed. The majority will be anxious, tense, and concerned. The challenge is how to make these guests feel safe in your hotel or venue. If one can make a person relax, not only will they be loyal, the odds are that they will also spend more in the hotel: at dinner, on room service, at the bar. Ken McCulloch, the great entrepreneurial hotelier and founder of Malmaison, believes that his hotels had appeal as their design and service made people feel relaxed and special. It allowed them to be uninhibited, as if they were in their own homes. If a hotel, he will argue, can make someone feel relaxed through a mix of design and service, then they will be loyal in return and return time and again.

The argument is simple: service must sit at the heart of any strategy to build good sustainable business in hospitality.

CHAPTER 8

Nothing Is More Important Than Trust and Relationships

The statement "nothing is more important than trust and relationships" is such an obvious comment but so many business strategies and philosophies in recent years have been arguably arrogant at times, communicating in an ever more process-led narrative and with less personal connection.

It is an approach where the negative consequences are becoming increasingly accepted and reversed as many seek to reconnect with the customer, to build a personal connection once again. It is hardly a shock to suggest that stronger businesses are built through good relationships and trust; yet still so many businesses operate through calls centers and automated systems which leave customers confused and frustrated.

The reason? Of course, a mix of cost, systems, and efficiencies. However, as Disney noted earlier, it is important not to view customer service and experience as a cost but as an economic asset. However, it should not require one of the world's leading companies to say the obvious. It is also a harder issue to unravel as, in truth, the world has become increasingly competitive so margins have become tighter, and every business strategy team looks at how they can make small percentage points of difference to maximize returns.

At the end of the day, it does come down to how important each business views possessing a personal relationship with their customers or clients. Great service is an expense which one needs to consider for the return on investment, and also how it does truly impact on developing customer loyalty and spend.

Consider for a moment a few points:

- How you do like automated services? Research has indicated that the majority are often left confused and frustrated (63).
- Should the use of technology replace the human touch, and shouldn't the first impression be personal rather than automated?
- In 2018, the Edelman Trust Barometer (64) noted that: The demise of confidence is driven primarily by a significant drop in trust in platforms, notably search engines and social media. Sixty three percent of respondents say they do not know how to tell good journalism from rumor or falsehoods or if a piece of news was produced by a respected media organization. This lack of faith has also led to an inability to identify the truth.
- In 2020, it noted that: "A majority of respondents in every developed market do not believe they will be better off in five years' time, and more than half of respondents globally believe that capitalism in its current form is now doing more harm than good in the world."
- Aviva, the leading insurance company, noted that automated systems do not generate trust. They note (65): "As innovation and automation increases, so does the debate around its trustworthiness. Would you go to a robot doctor? Would you entrust your child's education to a robo-teacher? Would you feel safe in a driverless car? Many wouldn't."

To be effective in building trust with a guest or customer, then service does matter. If lost trust is to be regained once again, then of course, companies are going to have to exceed expectations; it will not just happen without more investment in creating either stronger personal connections or higher service levels, even through technology. The prevailing view is that the aforementioned has been a natural stage in evolution, discovering how technology can work effectively, but the challenge is to find the right balance between technological advancement and higher service standards. There are many examples when personal service can be improved through technological advancement.

The real question at the heart is how do businesses build strong "fan" bases and trust with those they serve?

Forbes (66) noted in an article in 2019 that:

The 2019 Edelman Brand Trust Survey revealed only 39% believe tech companies put welfare of customers ahead of profits. What's more, although 81% say trust impacts their purchasing decisions, only a third of people say they trust the brands they buy from. And, 41% say they don't trust brands' marketing communications to be accurate or truthful.

The article went on to say: "According to Edelman's survey, 45% of consumers would never trust a brand again after it displays unethical behaviour or is involved in a scandal, and 40% say they'd stop buying from that brand altogether."

A few more thoughts for consideration:

- When hosting a dinner party at home, would you not greet in person your guest at the door and make sure they are welcomed warmly and made to feel both safe and comfortable?
- Is it a fair expectation that the first impression should be personable and with a human touch? Is it likely that a human interaction will be more effective than an automated system?
- Are you more likely to forgive a human error when accompanied by a genuine apology rather than a technical note or e-mail?

The Challenge Is to Rebuild Trust

Does it really matter if a customer does have trust in a business?

A report in 2018 by Accenture noted that in the modern world, it does very much matter (67) and estimated that over $2.5 trillion per year was lost through lack of trust and a potential 41 percent loss of clients. This does make every business have more vulnerability than should be the case. It also noted that 34 percent find more value in services which learn of their needs through personal services.

However, the issue goes deeper as Accenture noted that:

Those that succeed will hit a sweet spot whereby customers will be willing to share more personal insights into their world in return for greater value and the confidence that their data is protected. (67)

The equation is simple: Trust = greater potential data, information, and sales opportunities.

The issue of trust has often not been taken seriously enough across all walks of life. Trust has been eroded through a whole number of factors over the last 20 years.

- There is little doubt the relatively new concept of "fake news" has eroded trust in the media. Both "fake news" and "alternative facts" have become almost accepted issues, and many are showing signs of turning away from leading news channels.
- There is little doubt that politics did lose trust with a series of scandals over the years.
- For companies, as already noted, consumers do lack trust in the behaviors of many and as already noted, millennial employees do not trust in the business ethics of some their own companies.
- In the modern world the issue gets heightened with the fact the personal data is held by those who are sometimes not trusted. In one report in 2019 (68), it was noted that in one year, there were 4.5 billion records compromised.
- The same report stated that "86% of consumers wished that businesses would tell them how their data is being used, and 91% reported that they would be more likely to trust a business that was transparent"

Trust Is the Major Battleground

Trust is the battleground that every business today does need to win. In simple terms:

- It lays down a basis for a good relationship between a client/ customer and the business. It provides an informal license to trade successfully and also to be able to achieve higher sales revenues per customer.
- Trust can only be rebuilt by companies connecting on a stronger level with their customers. Service can and will play a crucial role in establishing this platform.
- However, it is deeper. Companies need to build authentic ties with communities and in social initiatives. As many of the emerging generations have changed their focus toward the importance of both "local and global" causes, so they will naturally lean toward those companies that share this outlook.
- Although the world today has never been more connected, more transparent, and open, it is the almost old-fashioned techniques and values which may well prove to be of most importance.
  - Customers who trust and believe in a brand or company become the best marketing tool for that company. They become the ambassadors for building trust once again.
  - The same can be said in relation to employees and how local communities do trust in an organization. The local community becomes a major advocate for the company as an employer and as a business.
- In a world which is increasingly transparent and vulnerable, it is important to almost behave in the same way: with vulnerability, unafraid to talk with openness and honesty. The same is asked of leaders. There needs to be far less spin and more honesty.

In a world which is aiming to rebuild, it is fascinating that in so many ways the previous values could also be related to the rebuilding of economies after World War II. Of course, that situation was far worse: 60 million dead. It was estimated that in 1945, most Europeans were living off 1,000 calories per day and it acted as an accelerator in new science and technology. It lay the ground for the modern computers, for the advent of penicillin, and it brought together a new philosophy that each society needed to care for its vulnerable again. In the United Kingdom, it led to the radical Labour Government, under Clement Atlee, which founded the NHS.

The war also advanced the importance of women: in France and Italy, women were given the vote. In his Four Freedoms speech of January 1941, President Roosevelt talked of a new and more just world, with freedom of speech, expression, and religion, and freedom from want and fear. Traditional old-fashioned "empires" did crumble. The British pulled out of India in 1947, leaving behind two new countries of India and Pakistan. Burma, Sri Lanka, and Malaysia followed the road of independence not long after. The Dutch fought a losing war but finally conceded independence to Indonesia, the former Dutch East Indies, in 1949. France tried to regain its colonies in Indochina but was forced out in 1954 after a humiliating defeat at the hands of Vietnamese forces. The Europeans' African empires crumbled in the 1950s and early 1960s. The United Nations grew from 51 nations in 1945 to 189 by the end of the century.

There are clear parallels between the eras and many similar desires. As the world becomes ever more advanced, it may well be that the base truths never really change. People do desire:

- Strong local communities and a caring society
- Real collaboration within communities and with countries, without control
- A desire for greater freedoms, less control: more openness and transparency
- A desire for trust in leadership and in strong ethics, behaviors

The challenge is to rebuild trust in a world which is under increased pressure. It is not hard to be achieved. It can easily be done but it does need a genuine new focus on the importance of relationships and trust.

Trust can be regained through four key actions/areas of focus:

- Customers believing in the motives and actions of the business. This can be built through better communications than has been the case in recent times and through strong service ethics. Over the last 20 years, there has been many column

inches devoted to communications and so often it is ineffec-
tual and missing in real agendas. Communication has often
failed and been at the heart of the erosion of trust. Maybe the
most obvious example is over the presentations for the Iraq
War by both the U.S. and U.K. governments which did leave
many bemused and angry. However, the communications of
many businesses too have been widely mistrusted and
poor in content.

- Delivering on promise with care. Customers will forgive
  errors and mistake is if there is genuine care shown. However,
  the hard truth is that most relationships between a business
  and a customer is over a task or transaction, so how this is
  delivered is crucial.
- A belief in the ethical approach of a business, in its honesty,
  fairness, and authenticity.
- By the company possessing a clear mission and purpose.

These are four strong pillars in which companies can rebuild trust and
in truth, should always exist.

CHAPTER 9

An Industry of Hope and Optimism, One Which Can Break Barriers

The hospitality industry is reflective of society and the consumer. The industry has a genuine opportunity as it is able to play a number of key roles on a number of levels. As has been outlined, hospitality does play a key social role in being a major pillar in society, in the communities that it serves, and in the multiracial multicultural teams that it employs. It is one of the major employers across most societies and plays a highly influential role both within the majority of economies and within societies across the world.

The hospitality industry has a far bigger role to play in modern society which is often not recognized. This book has looked at a whole range of factors from culture, to the social, to diets and food, to diversity and inclusion, to the importance of service. Hospitality also has the power to lead in environmental development, support economies, and influence the consumer through the power of its food, its eco-systems, and its approach to tourism.

When one writes about environmental sustainability, most will naturally think of climate change and global warming. These are major issues which do require serious changes in the approach of big business and in government policies. However, hospitality too has its role to play. It can play a role not only in good environmental practice but also in engaging travellers to think differently about the destinations to which they are prepared to travel.

The impact on the environment has become of increasing importance to many consumers and travellers. Increasingly consumer attitudes are favoring environmentally responsible businesses. This has extended to travelling, where consumers are considering environmental issues when making travel plans and purchases. Moreover, hospitality does sit at the heart of international tourism.

In 2019, France remained the most visited country with close to 90 million visitors, followed by Spain (69).

The most visited countries (69a) are:

- France: 86.9 million visitors
- Spain: 81.8 million
- United States: 76.9 million
- China: 60.7 million
- Italy: 58.3 million
- Mexico: 39.3 million
- United Kingdom: 37.7 million
- Turkey: 37.6 million
- Germany: 37.5 million
- Thailand: 35.4 million

It is not hard to see the natural common threads through all these major destinations: great tourism infrastructures, great food, and history.

Interestingly, the countries which have shown the greatest increase in tourism levels in 2019 were the following:

Fastest growing countries (territories) for tourism (69):

1. Myanmar 40.2 percent
2. Puerto Rico 31.2 percent
3. Iran 27.9 percent
4. Uzbekistan 27.3 percent
5. Montenegro 21.4 percent
6. Egypt 21.1 percent
7. Vietnam 16.2 percent
8. Philippines 15.1 percent
9. Maldives 14.9 percent
10. Bahamas 14.6 percent
11. Qatar 14.5 percent
12. Armenia 14.4 percent
13. South Korea 14.4 percent

14. Turkey 14.0 percent
15. Bosnia and Herzegovina 13.7 percent
16. Tunisia 13.6 percent
17. Laos 11.5 percent
18. Azerbaijan 11.4 percent
19. Israel 10.5 percent
20. Lithuania 10.1 percent
21. Kazakhstan 10.0 percent

The Iran Factor

The fact that Iran is third on the list will surprise many, especially given the fact that it has been one of the most controversial regimes over the past 40 years. However, in many ways, this does illustrate one of the underlying arguments throughout the text that many today are less concerned about the politics but want to understand and touch the history of the region, understand its culture and food styles. However, it is important to note that it is not western tourists who are the core audience for tourism to Iran but from Iraq, Azerbaijan, Afghanistan, Turkey, and Pakistan. Iran is investing more into its tourism infrastructure and last year's figures accounted for 6.5 percent of GDP.

Despite the political tensions, it would not be a surprise to see greater growth in tourism to Iran as there has been a renewed interest in its long history, and its food styles have become increasingly popular all around the world.

In December 2019, Airbnb released a report (70) outlining what they believed would be the most popular destinations, pre-Covid-19, and noted a trend toward eco-conscious destinations. The list was based on the highest percentage increase in bookings via their platform and it would be unlikely that many would be able to come even close to being correct to guessing the locations with the highest percentage leaps. Their leading top 10 destinations forecast included:

1. Milwaukee, WI, USA. Not many could have forecast this city being the number 1 forecast but Milwaukee is set to host the 2020 Democratic National Convention. Located on Lake Michigan,

the city is also home to various cultural museums and to over 105 miles of bike lanes. Milwaukee had an enormous 729 percent rise in bookings for 2020 compared to 2019.

2. Bilbao, Spain. Bilbao won European City of the Year in 2018, and for a good reason. Home to a lively restaurant scene and striking architecture, this city has quickly risen in the ranks to become one of the hottest spots in all of Spain. Bilbao had a 402 percent rise in interest for 2020.

3. Buriarm, Thailand. Buriarm is famed for its history and beauty.

4. Sunbury, Australia. Sunbury saw a 356 percent rise in booking for 2020 and is well known for both its vineyards and Victorian architecture.

5. Romania. Romania is building a strong reputation for its ecotourism structure and of course its dark history.

6. Xi'an, China, the birthplace of Chinese civilization and home to the famed Terracotta Army.

7. Eugene, OR, USA, known to be a culinary destination.

8. Luxemburg, a small country but still unknown and with many great medieval castles.

9. Guadalajara, Mexico, known for its festivals and museums

10. Vanuatu, located nearly 2,000 miles east of Australia and consists of over 80 islands, with over 100 native languages across them

The common thread amongst the prior list is a mix of strong cultures, history, great restaurants and food styles, and a growing focus on sustainability. Given all the aforementioned, it is clear that strong sustainable development is an important part of hospitality's jigsaw.

Originally, the focus on the environment has been understandably on those big businesses which do create pollution to the environment. However, the topic has become far wider and it is very clear that economies are influenced by their approach to the environment and eco-tourism. The hospitality industry has become a core industry as it is able to highlight what can be good practice and be strong role models for sustainable change. Just as hotels can play a major role in cultural sustainability, so they can also play a key role in good practice in managing a balance between environment, community, and sustainability.

There are so many hotels and restaurants which are situated in locations of beauty, stunning landscapes, in historical cities too where travellers want to escape to. The challenge for hoteliers and resorts is how to maintain the ecological balance between the need for development and the need to protect the environment.

It is clear from the preceding results that consumers want to travel to locations which can bring together the balance of modern facilities, great landscapes, history, and good food styles. The industry will naturally have to work hard at how it can manage the balance between customers, who are seeking ever more advanced luxury experiences, and the need to stay true to the environment. It will naturally be an area of growing tension with a need for new innovation.

The main environmental impacts due to the hospitality industry are CO_2 emissions, CFC emissions, noise, smoke, smells, health of staff, waste energy, waste water, waste food, waste disposal, agricultural ecology, purchasing policies, transportation policies, sale of souvenirs made from endangered species, and location of hotels in fragile locations. All these areas are having new solutions found with the aid of new technology and there is little doubt that the industry can become a role model for others.

Breaking Down Barriers

As the title to this chapter suggests, maybe one of the most important areas for consideration is how the hospitality industry can play a positive role in educating travellers and customers on the great variety which the world does possess; and in doing so gradually break down traditional barriers.

As all the aforementioned statistics do suggest, one of the common threads through tourism is the attraction of great hospitality mixed with culture, tradition, and great food styles. It is no coincidence that the leading countries for tourism include France, Spain, United States, China, and Italy. They all bring together great food, hospitality, and culture. As the learnings from these countries can be replicated across other countries, so the customer experience will naturally improve and barriers will be broken down. Tourism is going to be increasingly important to nearly all economies in the future. It will be important, of course, to economies, but also in developing a deeper understanding and knowledge. Hospitality and tourism bring people together, share experiences, create memories, immerse people in culture and history which can educate those that do visit. It is maybe a farfetched argument to say that hospitality and tourism can promote peace and prosperity but it can certainly create stronger understanding which breaks down barriers. According to research by the World Travel and Tourism Council (71) countries with a more open and sustainable tourism sector tend to be more peaceful.

One of the major changes, in recent times, has been the move from travellers wanting to seek great experiences which arguably caused many destinations to create experiences that the guest would want, rather than what was genuine and authentic. This has changed and the focus is far more on the guest seeking the genuine, authentic experience and with a far higher level of respect for local customs and traditions. The guest arguably used to seek a "manufactured" experience, but today seeks to find an experience which allows them to feel part of the local culture. Naturally, this creates more mutual respect, stronger care, and understanding across cultures.

> The power of tourism is to build peace and mutual understanding. This is an industry which puts a smile on the faces of people, those that are visiting and those that are hosting. It is an industry of hope and optimism.
>
> —Dr. Taleb Refai, Secretary General, UNWTO (72)

Hope and Optimism

It is an interesting point to raise after all the troubles and sadness that the industry will face following the Covid-19 crisis. All across the globe, the industry will need to fight its way out of a recession. However, there is genuine optimism to be found amongst many leaders who do see a new era arising and one where hospitality could be a strong force.

It is a well-known feature of the emerging generations in that they are seeking experiences: they view experiences over possessions. They seek both a strong work–life balance but also have a thirst to learn far more about the cultures around the world than previous generations have done. This can place hospitality right at the heart of these trends and provides a genuine opportunity for growth in the industry's importance.

The industry can play a positive role across countries, continents, societies, and communities in generating a strong understanding of global societies within safer and secure environments.

The Impact of Covid-19 on Cities

One of the interesting discussions at the time of writing, during Covid-19 crisis, is just how cities may be forced to change and adapt. More and more research is emerging that many do not want to return to their previous lifestyles: of commuting into cities, of public transport within cities; and working within the old offices that existed pre-Covid-19. The argument is that the Covid crisis has changed the need to work within offices and that many have learnt to live and work, through new technology, from their homes. In turn they have enjoyed the relationship that they have found within local communities. The argument of this moment is that it is going to be very hard to re-engage many teams to return to work in traditional office environments. Interestingly, this reluctance is not just with millennials and Gen Z but also with many senior players who too want to witness genuine change.

The counter argument is that hard economics will demand that life will return to a sense of normality and things do generally return to a natural normality.

Both arguments have merit and, in truth, businesses will find a new balance. As all the statistics noted precrisis, the level of disengagement and stress was already too high and there needed to be an adjustment. The lockdown period has arguably been a correction, and a balance will need to be found. However, it is very likely that cities will change as a result.

Some argue that the cities have been the center of the storm just as cities have always been the center of historical plagues. History will often show that it does take some considerable time to recover from such episodes. The difference this time is that many employees believe they can change their lifestyles and work pattern using technology. It is natural that many will argue that cities will decline but history has also shown that, although it takes time to recover, generally cities continue to grow. Cities will always be the base of power and authority; will always be where the great economic wealth will sit; and will therefore always attract the ambitious and aspirational.

However, it may change the investment focus and infrastructure within cities. Sustainability will become increasingly of importance. It is likely more pedestrian areas will be created and even many large skyscrapers and office will be turned into areas of accommodation, if work patterns do change. With sustainability in mind, there may well be more investment into the development of parks and natural areas of recreation.

It is always dangerous to write in a moment of crisis as so many emotions and opinions are hardened but it is a fair rationale to expect many cities to already be planning for another such occurrence, should one arise. Many felt they were underprepared as Covid-19 struck. All advanced economies will naturally be more prepared.

The real challenge, and unknown, is that it has been estimated that 95 percent of those that suffered with Covid-19 did operate professionally or live within urban areas. The view is that the crisis has served to also highlight the inequalities in society and the dangers that the disadvantaged do suffer. Given this, it is logical that both local and national governments will invest and work harder to ensure that urban environments will see a drive to lessen inequalities and be far more sustainable and environmentally stronger locations in the future.

At the end of the day, companies and economies need to rebuild. This will require thriving cities. There will need to be a change in emphasis in order to ensure greater safety and less inequality but cities will also need to change track in order to combat the desire of many toward rural locations so that they can attract the best talent back into the cities.

In short term, it is likely that cities will become less crowded and naturally the overall pace of life will slow. Local authorities will rethink their planning with a greater focus on how they engage visitors and people back into the centers. With less activity, even in the short term, it will naturally lead to the urban air being much cleaner and urban life less expensive. At the same time, cities will become safer environments. All this together will naturally see a revival in time of urban areas. They will come back but it will be different, and cities will be both smarter and more sustainable.

Overall, the key theme in this chapter is that life is changing, evolving and despite all the challenges to be faced in the immediate future, there is a belief that good can emerge from the dark times. The hospitality industry faces no few challenges in the major urban areas over the next 2 years, but it also has the new opportunity play a deeper and more important role across the world.

CHAPTER 10

Service Is Purpose

There is no doubting that most countries face a daunting and challenging time ahead as businesses and economies are rebuilt. However, there is optimism about the long-term future and a strong belief that hospitality can play an important and central role in the future, in social and cultural sustainability, in tourism, in economies all across the world, and in breaking down barriers. It could, all together, mark the start of a new era for hospitality with both sustainability and service sitting very much at its heart.

In the United Kingdom, especially, service has never been a respected concept. It has been seen as being secondary but there is little doubt that service is growing and becoming more important all the time. Service to others, as a concept, is once again growing. There has been a deep frustration with the perceived self-interest of politicians and businesses, a frustration which is seeing the balance change with many in the emerging generations now believing that service to others is a central theme. It creates a natural purpose and definition to life.

The millennials are showing the highest volunteer rates of any generation: they value helping others, buying food that's eco-friendly, supporting products and organizations that are socially conscious, and wanting to do good in their community and in the world. Companies all across the world are going to be asked, by consumers and employees: do you meet this criterion?

For hospitality, this does mark a significant opportunity, arguably the greatest opportunity it has faced in its long and proud history. Hospitality companies have shown during the Covid-19 crisis that they can play an active role in communities, helping the vulnerable and supporting those who face food poverty. Hospitality today also has a stronger and genuine purpose in how it can interact and operate with communities, how it can tell the story of local cultures and histories, and how it can talk to global audiences and break down traditional barriers. Hospitality can operate with genuine purpose as it can be a leading role model in how it serves others.

"Chefs have the power to change the world."

It has long been argued that chefs do possess the power to create genuine social change if they could really come together and work as one. It is food which is the one true universal language, it is argued, and food which brings people together to break down barriers. Of course, there is sound logic to the argument but, in truth, is unlikely to happen as, first, chefs are skilled in their craft with a passion for their skill rather than possessing any passion of social activism. Second, restaurants are often working to low margins and do create great wealth to lead any global change.

A restaurant though is a stage which can educate and break down barriers. This is an important asset in itself.

The previous saying really should be that "hospitality has the power to change the world" for it does, both locally and globally. Service can really be purpose for, in a world which has been dominated by anxiety, stress, and tension, it can bring relief and break down traditional tensions.

Leadership, of course, will sit right at the heart of the change. It will be hospitality leaders who will dictate the future direction of businesses and hopefully in the knowledge that their businesses possess the genuine ability to create real difference and become a role model industry. Just as leadership sits at the heart of the change, so leadership will be determined by the behaviors and ethics that they will allow to work by.

As has been well documented, the challenge now is to rebuild the lost trust that has developed in all leaders over the last 20 years. Leadership has been called into account and it will be how business leaders are able to think with greater breadth which will allow for that trust to be rebuilt successfully. The demands of a new sustainable agenda will be to once again think more deeply about the way their business behaves with the consumer, the employee, and the local community. Leaders will be expected to act with greater purpose and greater care and with the interests of a bigger agenda in future.

This is the opportunity for hospitality to be a role model industry which can support real change across so many areas. The industry has long been known and criticized for lagging behind others in a number of areas: in technology, in diversity and inclusion, in working with communities. Now it needs to catch up and become a genuine leader where it matters. This can be an exciting new era for the industry but only if it takes it. If the industry has lagged behind previously, then it needs to accept that it has work to do, does need to change, to bring in fresh ideas, new innovation, and thinking.

For so long, the industry has felt as almost a second-tier industry. It has now the opportunity to become one of real importance and one which can pave the path to a stronger future.

It can be an industry that does bring hope, change, and optimism to communities all across the world. It is time for the industry to lead, to be a beacon of hope and good, to bring people together and be a home for all talent.

References

1. Quincy Seale. Uplifting Quotes - https://keepinspiring.me/uplifting-quotes-for-difficult-times/

2. BrainyQuote. www.brainyquote.com/quotes/mark_twain

2a. EP Business in Hospitality 2020. www.epinsights.co.uk

2b. EP Business in Hopsitality. Carrie Wicks, Uncut and In Conversation 2020. Youtube - https://youtube.com/watch?v=wk5f4CaTT_Q

3. Quincy Seale. Uplifting Quotes. https://keepinspiring.me/uplifting-quotes-for-difficult-times/

3a. 2020 Edelman Trust Barometer January 19, 2020. https://edelman.com/trustbarometer

4. Wikipedia. The Economy of Nigeria.

5. BrainyQuote. Gordon Brown. https://brainyquote.com/quotes/gordon_brown_758393?src=t_financial_crisis

6. BrainyQuote. Steve Bannon. https://brainyquote.com/quotes/steve_bannon_788612?src=t_financial_crisis

7. Caleb Silver. "10+ years Later; Lessons from the 2008 Financial Crisis" Investopedia www.investopedia.com

8. Caleb Silver. "10+ years Later; Lessons from the 2008 Financial Crisis" Investopedia www.investopedia.com

9. The Daily Telegraph 24th January 2010. *"1.3m People have Lost their Jobs in the Recession."* https://telegraph.co.uk/finance/jobs/7066404/1.3m-people-have-lost-their-jobs-in-the-recession-finds-report.html

10. Britain's Healthiest Workplace by Vitality 2019. https://vitality.co.uk/business/healthiest-workplace/findings/

11. Andrew. J.H. Spring 2018. "The Next Phase of Business Sustainability." *Stanford Social Innovation Review.* https://ssir.org/articles/entry/the_next_phase_of_business_sustainability

12. Andrew. J.H. Spring 2018. "The Next Phase of Business Sustainability." Stanford *Social Innovation Review.* https://ssir.org/articles/entry/the_next_phase_of_business_sustainability

13. Andrew. J.H. Spring 2018. "The Next Phase of Business Sustainability." *Stanford Social Innovation Review.* https://ssir.org/articles/entry/the_next_phase_of_business_sustainability

14. Ecole Hoteliere de Lausanne www.ehl.edu

15. Robert Half May 25, 2017. "The Changing Nature of a CEO." https://roberthalf.co.uk/advice/c-suite/changing-nature-ceo

16. Larry Elliott, The Guardian November 3, 2016. "The Bank of England got if Both Wrong and Right." https://theguardian.com/business/2016/nov/03/bank-of-england-uk-economy-analysis-interest-rates-inflation-brexit-vote

17. The House of Commons. https://parliament.uk/business/commons/

18. Kristen Bialik and Richard Fry February 14, 2019. "Millennial Life: How young adulthood today compares with prior generations." https://pewsocialtrends.org/essay/Millennial-life-how-young-adulthood-today-compares-with-prior-generations/

19. Spencer Stuart Claudius Hildebrand, Robert Stark and Jim Citrin 2018

19a. Aaron Schnoor February 6, "The Problem of the Ageing CEO." https://medium.com/the-intelligence-of-everything/the-problem-of-the-aging-ceo-e09e8d21bb65

20. Finextra. April 29, 2020. "Barclays CEO signals the end of the Skyscraper and the Birth of the Branch." https://finextra.com/newsarticle/35731/covid-19-barclays-ceo-signals-end-of-the-skyscraper-and-rebirth-of-the-branch

21. Wikipedia The Eurovision Song Contest. https://en.wikipedia.org/wiki/Eurovision_Song_Contest

22. Beyond Investment Group. 2019. "A Record Growth." https://beyondinvestmentsgroup.com/tourism-analysis-greece2019

23. Statista Research Dept. February 5, 2020. https://statista.com/statistics/628849/tourism-total-contribution-to-gdp-italy-share/

24. Wikipedia. https://en.wikipedia.org/wiki/Tourism_in_France

25. Trading Economics. https://tradingeconomics.com/united-states/tourism-revenues

26. Susannah Griffin. October 1, 2019. "The Importance of Sport to the UK economy." https://wealthandfinance-news.com/the-importance-of-sports-to-the-uk-economy/

27. Tome Morrissey-Swan. June 18, 2018. "How Curry became Britain's Favourite Home-Cooked Dish." https://telegraph.co.uk/food-and-drink/news/curry-became-britains-favourite-home-cooked-dish/

28. Clay's Handbook of environmental health edited by Stephen, B. 2016.

29. Alisha Haridasani Gupta. December 17, 2019. *"California Companies are Rushing to Find Female Board Members."* https://nytimes.com/2019/12/17/us/california-boardroom-gender-quota.html

30. Accountancy Daily. Amy Austin. November 4, 2016. "Number of BAME Directors in FTSE 100 Stalls at 8%." https://accountancydaily.co/number-bame-directors-ftse-100-stalls-8

31. Accountancy Daily. December 5, 2019. Pat Sweet "FTSE 100 failing at Boardroom Ethnic Diversity." https://accountancydaily.co/ftse-100-failing-boardroom-ethnic-diversity

32. Catalyst. January 16, 2019. "Number of Fortune 500 boards with over 40% diversity doubled since 2012." https://catalyst.org/media-release/number-of-fortune-500-boards-with-over-40-percent-diversity-doubled-since-2012/

33. Marcus Noland, Tyler Moran and Barbara Kotschwar. February 8, 2016. "Peteson Institute of Internatonal Economics." https://piie.com/newsroom/press-releases/new-peterson-institute-research-over-21000-companies-globally-finds-women

34. PWC Diversity Global Annual Report. 2019. https://pwc.com/gx/en/about/global-annual-review-2019/diversity-and-inclusion.html

35. McKinsey. "Delivering through Diversity." https://efm-berlinale.de/en/diversity-inclusion/resources/delivering-through-diversity/delivering-through-diversity.html

36. The Millennial Survey report 2019 Deloittes. https://www2.deloitte.com/content/dam/Deloitte/global/Documents/About-Deloitte/deloitte-2019-Millennial-survey.pdf

37. Socialtalent.com "9 Companies around the World Embracing Diversity in a Big Way." https://socialtalent.com/solution/corporate

38. The Drum. Minda Smiley. March 2, 2017. "P&G Launches #weseeequal Campaign." https://thedrum.com/news/2017/03/02/pg-launches-weseeequal-campaign-ahead-international-women-s-day

39. The Daily Telegraph. Guy Kelly. May 24, 2016. "A (Nearly) Complete Glossary of gender identities for your next census." https://telegraph.co.uk/men/the-filter/a-nearly-complete-glossary-of-gender-identities-for-your-next-ce/

40. John F Kennedy Library and Museum. https://jfklibrary.org/learn/education/teachers/curricular-resources/elementary-school-curricular-resources/ask-not-what-your-country-can-do-for-you

41. EP Business in Hospitality. www.epinsights.co.uk

42. The Vegan Society. https://vegansociety.com/news/media/statistics

43. "The Age of Veganism." Boriania Slabakova January 7, 2020. https://healthcareers.co/vegan-statistics/

44. The Guardian. Damian Carrington. May 7, 2018. "Avoiding Meat and Diary is the Single Biggest Way to Reduce your Impact on Earth." https://theguardian.com/environment/2018/may/31/avoiding-meat-and-dairy-is-single-biggest-way-to-reduce-your-impact-on-earth

45. Mintel. November 2018. "More than half of Meat-Free New Products Launches in UK Carried a Vegan Claim in 2017." https://mintel.com/press-centre/food-and-drink/more-than-half-of-all-meat-free-new-product-launches-in-the-uk-carry-a-vegan-claim-1

46. EP Business in Hospitality. www.epinsights.co.uk

47. The Food Industry Association. October 22, 2019. "Rick Stein How the Rise of "Flexitarians" is Powering Plant-Based Sales." https://fmi.org/blog/view/fmi-blog/2019/10/22/how-the-rise-of-flexitarians-is-powering-plant-based-sales)

48. Forbes. Oliver Garrett. September 3, 2019. "Beyond Meat will Crash When Investors Realise What It's Really Selling." https://forbes.com/sites/oliviergarret/2019/09/03/beyond-meat-will-crash-when-investors-realize-what-its-really-selling/#360e44f45ea2

49. The St.Andrews Economist. Lucy Wright. Febraury 21, 2020. "Economics and the Environment: The Rise of Veganism." https://thestandrewseconomist.com/2020/02/21/economics-and-the-environment-the-rise-of-veganism/

50. University of Oxford. March 16, 2017. "Social Eating Connects Communities." http://ox.ac.uk/news/2017-03-16-social-eating-connects-communities#

51. The Atlantic. Cody Delistraty. July 14, 2016. "The Importance of Eating Together." https://theatlantic.com/health/archive/2014/07/the-importance-of-eating-together/374256/

52. EP Business in Hospitality. www.epinsights.co.uk

53. David Read. Prestige Purchasing. https://prestige-purchasing.com/staff-member/david-read/

54. CNN. Alaa Elassar. November 19, 2019. "Amazon Deforestation Rat Eits Highest Level in Over a Decade." https://edition.cnn.com/2019/11/19/americas/brazil-deforestation-amazon-2019-trnd/index.html

55. Wikipedia. TGI Fridays. https://en.wikipedia.org/wiki/TGI_Fridays

56. Harvard Business Review. Bruce Jones. Febraury 28, 2018. "3 Principles Disney Uses to Enhance Customer Experiences." https://hbr.org/sponsored/2018/02/3-principles-disney-uses-to-enhance-customer-experience

57. EP Business in Hospitality. www.epinsights.co.uk

58. EP Business in Hospitality. www.epinsights.co.uk

59. New York Times. June 10, 2020. Nate Cohn and Kevin Quealy "How Public Opinion has Moved on Black Lives Matter." https://nytimes.com/interactive/2020/06/10/upshot/black-lives-matter-attitudes.html

60. Monmouth University Polling Institute. June 2, 2020. "Protestors Anger Justified Even If Actions May not be." https://monmouth.edu/polling-institute/reports/monmouthpoll_us_060220/

61. Goodreads. https://goodreads.com/quotes/tag/movement

62. BrainyQuote. https://brainyquote.com/quotes/winston_churchill_165927

63. The Independent. Grant Bailey. October 11, 2018. "Millions of British People are Confused by Automated Services, Survey Claims." https://independent.co.uk/extras/lifestyle/automated-services-shops-hotels-self-checkout-british-people-confusing-a8578911.html

64. 2020 Edelman Trust Barometer. https://edelman.com/trustbarometer

65. Aviva. July 16, 2018. *The Decline of Trust.* https://aviva.com/newsroom/perspectives/2018/07/the-decline-of-trust/

66. Forbes/Michael Fertik. November 26, 2019. "How to Get Customers to Trust You." https://forbes.com/sites/michaelfertik/2019/11/26/how-to-get-customers-to-trust-you/#68a4456bf8d6

67. Social Media Week. Erica Perry. Febraury 6, 2018. "Lack of Trust Costs Brands $2.5 Trillion Per Year." https://socialmediaweek.org/blog/2018/02/lack-trust-costs-brands-2-5-trillion-per-year-study/

68. 10 to 8. "How the Customer Trust Crisis Might be Affecting your Business." https://10to8.com/blog/customer-trust-crisis/

69. The Independent. Helen Coffey. Febraury 3, 2020. "The World's fastest growing tourist destinations from Uzbeskistan to Iran." https://independent.co.uk/travel/news-and-advice/tourist-countries-popular-uzbekistan-iran-myanmar-egypt-visitor-numbers-a9314311.html

69a. Big Seven Travel. January 2, 2019. https://bigseventravel.com/2019/01/most-visited-countries-2019/

70 The Business Insider. Dominic- Madori Davis. December 25, 2019. "World's top 20 travel destinations for 2020." https://businessinsider.com/airbnb-top-trending-places-to-travel-worldwide-2020?r=US&IR=T#20-maastricht-netherlands-1

71 World Travel Tourism Council. Insights. https://wttc.org/Research/Insights/other-research/tourism-as-a-driver-of-peace

72 Chemonics. Maysa Shahateet. November 28, 2017. "Finding Balance: Cultural Preservation and Tourism." https://chemonics.com/blog/finding-balance-cultural-preservation-tourism/

About the Author

Chris Sheppardson is the founder of a leading hospitality consultancy—EP, Business in Hospitality (founded 2005)—which specializes in progressive thinking and in bringing together industry leaders to debate key issues of the day plus publishes regular articles on major topics. Chris is also the founder of Chess Partnership (founded 1998) which is a leading recruitment concern for senior appointments in hospitality. Chris has had previous books published in the fields of both hospitality and sport: *A Time of Change in Hospitality Leadership (2020) The Luxury Hotels of London* (1991), *Leadership and Entrepreneurship in the Hospitality Industry* (2011), *If Only* (2015), *For the Love of the Game* (2016).

Researcher—Iwona Drozdz, joined EP in 2019 and is a trained psychotherapist. Iwona conducted many of the interviews with industry leaders which are quoted within the body of the text.

Index

Accenture, 125, 126
Airbnb, 133
AI/technology, 52–53
Allied Market Research, 94
Atlee, Clement, 128

Baby Boomer generation, xix, xxiv, xx, 32, 42–44, 73, 74
Bannon, Steve, 3
Beef, 100
Beyond Meat (BYND), 94
Bilbao, 134
Birch Hotel, 15, 16, 61
Bistronomie, 56
Black, Asian, and minority ethnic (BAME), xxvi, 3, 51, 76–79
Black Lives Matter movement, 115
Blair, Tony, 21, 41, 45
British cuisine, 64
Brown, Gordon, 3
Burger King, 56
Buriarm, 134
Business, 121–122
  culture and, 29–32
  leadership, 50
  long-term, 117
  and politics, 42, 50
  role, 82, 86
  strategy, 5, 28, 123
  sustainability (See Sustainable business)

Chefs, 79, 87, 88, 95, 142
Chief executive officer (CEO), xxiv, 6, 9, 15, 23, 30, 31, 34, 35, 37, 38, 43, 44, 48, 105, 119
Churchill, Winston, 117
#CitizenG–United to being Globally Green, 15
Clean energy, 17
Climate change, 26, 99, 101, 131

Coffee, 101
Community
  AI and, 52–53
  to leadership, 22–23
  localism and, 44–46
Community, purpose, and contribution (CPC), 46–49
Conrad Hotels and Resorts, 27
Coronavirus (Covid-19), xiii, xiv, xvi, xvii, xxv, 1, 3, 7, 12, 18, 19, 23, 24, 34, 39, 44, 48, 49, 53, 68, 74, 77, 84, 86, 87, 112–115, 133, 136–139, 141
C-suite, xvii, xviii, 71, 78
Cuisine, xxviii, 57, 63, 64, 67
Cultural diversity, 67–69
Cultural fit, 71
Cultural sustainability, 55–59
  diversity, 67–69
  Eurovision Song Contest, 59–60
  and tourism, 60–67
Culture, 24, 48–49
  and business models, 29–32
  and community, 29, 42

Deforestation, 99–104
Deloitte Millennial Survey (2018), 79
Delteil, Christian, 55, 57
Diet, 89–90
Disney, 106–107, 118, 119, 123
Diversity, 13, 66–69, 72, 74–82, 131, 143

Economics, 26, 42
Economic sustainability, 1–7
  localism, 7–12
Edelman Trust Barometer, xxv, 124, 125
Elliott, Adam, 120
Empathy, 110–113, 120–122
Employees, re-engaging, 82–83

Environmental
  effects, 91
  impacts, 135
  regulations, 13
  and social issues, xxvi
  sustainability, xxii, xxvii, 1, 11, 16,
    131
  technology, 17
EP, 92, 97
Ethical Chefs Association (ECA), 87
Eugene, 134
Eurovision Song Contest, 59–60

Fait Maison, 56
Flexibility, 83
Food, 54–56, 63–67, 89
  chain, 98–99
  and deforestation, 99–104
  delivering, 112
  diet changes, 89–90
  poverty, 18, 87, 88, 97, 141
  service, xxii, 54, 63–66, 86, 97,
    101, 103
  social sustainability through, 95–98
  styles, 7, 42, 62, 63, 66, 133–135
  veganism, 91–95
Food Miles, 102
Forbes, 94, 125
Forecast, 133–134
France, 7, 55, 56, 60, 62, 63, 128,
    132, 135
French gastronomy, 56, 57
Fuelling Productivity, 97

Gender equality, 78
Genuine service, 113–114
Gen Z, xxi, 42, 44, 50, 93, 137
Globalization, 7, 8, 42, 58, 66, 80, 81
Gray, Michael, 111–112
Guadalajara, 134

Healthiest Companies research, 14
Heritage, 3, 53, 55, 59, 60, 62, 64
Hilton, 27
Home Made, 56
Hope and optimism, 136–137
Hospitality, xxiii–xxiv, 7, 8, 15, 18,
    23, 27, 31, 53, 55, 57, 63, 68,
    69, 75, 77, 79, 80, 85–89,
    95–97, 105, 108–110, 112,
    113, 116–118, 120, 122, 131,
    132, 134–137, 139, 141, 142
  empathy, 110–113, 120–122
  opportunity for, 53–54
  workplaces changes and, 85–88
Hotels, 2, 6, 7, 10, 15, 23, 27–32, 53,
    57, 61, 69, 86, 93, 109, 110,
    119, 121, 122, 134, 135
Human resources director (HRD),
    34, 35

Identity, 77
Indian cuisine, 67
Iran, 133–135

Japanese cuisine, 64
John Lewis Partnership, 71–72
Johnson, Boris, 50

Kett, Russell, 5, 10, 29, 31–32

Leadership, 118–119
  business, 50
  community to, 22–23
  priorities, 5
  service, 23–24, 107
  teams, 32–36
  workplaces changes, 79–80
Leaders, purpose of, 116–118
Localism, 7–12
  and communities, 44–46
London Edition Hotels, 122
Luxemburg, 134

McCulloch, Ken, 2, 122
McDonalds, 118
McKinsey, 79
Majority groups, 97
Major, John, 21
Managing director (MD), 34, 35,
    105, 111
Marks & Spencer, 103–104
May, Theresa, 21
Mergers & Acquisitions (M&A), 71
"MeToo" campaign, 76

Millennial generation, xxi, xxiii, xxiv, 7, 12, 16, 32, 41, 43, 44, 46, 50, 51, 72–79, 83, 84, 93, 114, 126, 137, 141
Milwaukee, 133–134
Minority, 77

Nasty Party, The, 21
Nigeria, xxv–xxvi
Norman, Archie, 119

Office for National Statistics (ONS), 11
Open communication, 82

Palm oil, 100
Penn, Chris, 15
Politics, 18, 21, 23–24, 26, 29, 42, 45, 46, 50–52, 59, 81, 126, 133
Poverty, 18, 87, 88, 97, 141
Procter & Gamble's (P&G) "We See Equal" Campaign, 80
Puglia, 61
PWC report, 77–78

Read, David, 98
Reagan, Ronald, 42
Relationships and trust, 123–129
Renewable energy, 17
Renewables, 101–102
Resorts, 5, 7, 15, 27, 29, 55, 57, 58, 60, 61, 109, 135
Restaurants, xxviii, 7, 13, 28, 31, 53–57, 63, 64, 66, 106, 108, 110, 111, 117, 118, 135, 142
Rethink/Reduce/Rese/Recycle model, 101–102
Rinck, Martin, 27
Ritz-Carlton, 113, 119
Romania, 134
Round Table on Responsible Soy (RTRS), 100
Round Table on Sustainable Palm Oil (RSPO), 101

Service, xxix–xxx, 62, 141–143
enhancement, 105
ethos, 23
leadership, 23–24, 107

Service and sustainable, 105–107
business, 114–115
change, 116
empathy, 110–113, 120–122
genuine, 113–114
leaders, purpose of, 116–118
SMEPS, 108–110
training and development, 118–120
Service, mission, employee engagement, productivity, and sustainability (SMEPS), 108–110
Silent Generation, 42
Singapore, 66–67
Social media, 52, 65, 109, 114, 124
Social renewal, 41
AI/technology, 52–53
community, purpose, and contribution (CPC), 46–49
generations, 41–44
hospitality opportunity, 53–54
localism and communities, 44–46
politics, 50–52
Social sustainability, 28–29
through food, 95–98
Socialtalent.com, 80
Society, 1, 15, 16, 23, 27, 41, 45, 52, 56, 59, 63–65, 68, 69, 73, 75, 77, 80, 82–84, 86, 88–90, 95, 97, 116, 131, 138
Soy, 100
Spedan Lewis, John, 72
Sunbury, 134
Supplier management, 103–104
Sustainability, xiii–xxvii
environmental, xxii, xxvii, 1, 11, 16, 131. *See also* Cultural sustainability; Economic sustainability; Social sustainability
Sustainable business, 13–21, 114–115
challenge, 36–39
and change, 24–27
community support, 22–23
culture and business models, 29–32
leadership teams, 32–36

service leadership, 23–24
social sustainability, 28–29

Tan, Abigail, 15, 16, 72
Tea, 101
TGI Fridays, 106
Thatcher, Margaret, 42
Tick-box approach, 3
Tourism, 58, 60–67, 132–136, 141
Training and development, 118–120
Transport, 102
Truffelli, Marco, 111, 112, 119
Trust and relationships, 123–129
2008/09 crash, xxi, xxii, xxiii, 3, 4, 8,
     9, 11, 12, 15, 16, 20, 22, 27,
     44, 49, 71, 84, 114

United Kingdom, 9, 17, 44, 45, 59,
     60, 62–64, 67, 72, 76, 81,
     84, 87, 90, 92, 93, 97, 115,
     128, 141
United States, 41, 44, 45, 60, 76, 90,
     92, 135

Value authenticity, 83
Vanuatu, 134
Veganism, 91–95
Verdura Resort, 61

Waste, 103
Woke agendas, xxiii, xxx
Work community, 82–83
Workplaces changes, 71–74
   challenges, 83–85
   employees, re-engaging,
     82–83
   and hospitality, 85–88
   leadership, 79–80
   millennials and inclusion,
     74–79
   new era, 80–82
Work that matters, 83
World Heritage, 64
World Travel and Tourism Council,
     136

Xi'an, 134

OTHER TITLES IN THE TOURISM AND HOSPITALITY MANAGEMENT COLLECTION

Betsy Bender Stringam, New Mexico State University, Editor

- *Food and Architecture* by Subhadip Majumder and Sounak Majumder
- *A Time of Change in Hospitality Leadership* by Chris Sheppardson
- *Improving Convention Center Management Using Business Analytics and Key Performance Indicators, Volume II* by Myles T. McGrane
- *Improving Convention Center Management Using Business Analytics and Key Performance Indicators, Volume I* by Myles T. McGrane
- *Cultural and Heritage Tourism and Management* by Tammie J. Kaufman
- *Coastal Tourism, Sustainability, and Climate Change in the Caribbean, Volume II* by Martha Honey, Kreg Ettenger and Samantha Hogenson
- *Coastal Tourism, Sustainability, and Climate Change in the Caribbean, Volume I* by Martha Honey, Kreg Ettenger and Samantha Hogenson
- *Marine Tourism, Climate Change, and Resilience in the Caribbean, Volume II* by Kreg Ettenger, Samantha Hogenson and Martha Honey
- *Marketing Essentials for Independent Lodging* by Pamela Lanier and Marie Lanier
- *Marine Tourism, Climate Change, and Resiliency in the Caribbean, Volume I* by Kreg Ettenger, Samantha Hogenson and Martha Honey
- *Catering and Convention Service Survival Guide in Hotels and Casinos* by Lisa Lynn Backus and Patti J. Shock

Concise and Applied Business Books

The Collection listed above is one of 30 business subject collections that Business Expert Press has grown to make BEP a premiere publisher of print and digital books. Our concise and applied books are for...

- Professionals and Practitioners
- Faculty who adopt our books for courses
- Librarians who know that BEP's Digital Libraries are a unique way to offer students ebooks to download, not restricted with any digital rights management
- Executive Training Course Leaders
- Business Seminar Organizers

Business Expert Press books are for anyone who needs to dig deeper on business ideas, goals, and solutions to everyday problems. Whether one print book, one ebook, or buying a digital library of 110 ebooks, we remain the affordable and smart way to be business smart. For more information, please visit www.businessexpertpress.com, or contact sales@businessexpertpress.com.